GACE

Science

Practice Questions

I0889223

Mometrix

TEST PREPARATION

DEAR FUTURE EXAM SUCCESS STORY

First of all, **THANK YOU** for purchasing Mometrix study materials!

Second, congratulations! You are one of the few determined test-takers who are committed to doing whatever it takes to excel on your exam. **You have come to the right place.** We developed these practice tests with one goal in mind: to deliver you the best possible approximation of the questions you will see on test day.

Standardized testing is one of the biggest obstacles on your road to success, which only increases the importance of doing well in the high-pressure, high-stakes environment of test day. Your results on this test could have a significant impact on your future, and these practice tests will give you the repetitions you need to build your familiarity and confidence with the test content and format to help you achieve your full potential on test day.

Your success is our success

We would love to hear from you! If you would like to share the story of your exam success or if you have any questions or comments in regard to our products, please contact us at **800-673-8175** or **support@mometrix.com**.

Thanks again for your business and we wish you continued success!

Sincerely,
The Mometrix Test Preparation Team

Printed in the United States of America

Table of Contents

Practice Test #1

Refer to the following for question 1:

A sixth-grade science teacher tells her students that they will have a seismologist studying plate tectonics come to class. She has a group of early-intermediate English learners in her class. The seismologist will discuss what causes earthquakes, the effects of earthquakes, and any questions students might have on the topic.

1. One student wants to know what causes the shaking that occurs with an earthquake. What answer would the seismologist likely give to that student?

a. Static deformation
b. Seismic waves
c. Compression waves
d. Continental drift

2. Which of the following common household products is NOT correctly matched with the chemical associated with it?

a. Vinegar and acetic acid
b. Glass cleaner and sodium hypochlorite
c. Baking soda and sodium bicarbonate
d. Rubbing alcohol and isopropanol

3. Which of the following describes the process skill of concluding?

a. Explaining or interpreting observations
b. Making a determination based on the results of a controlled experiment
c. Reading an instrument during an experiment
d. Listing similarities and differences between two objects

Refer to the following for question 4:

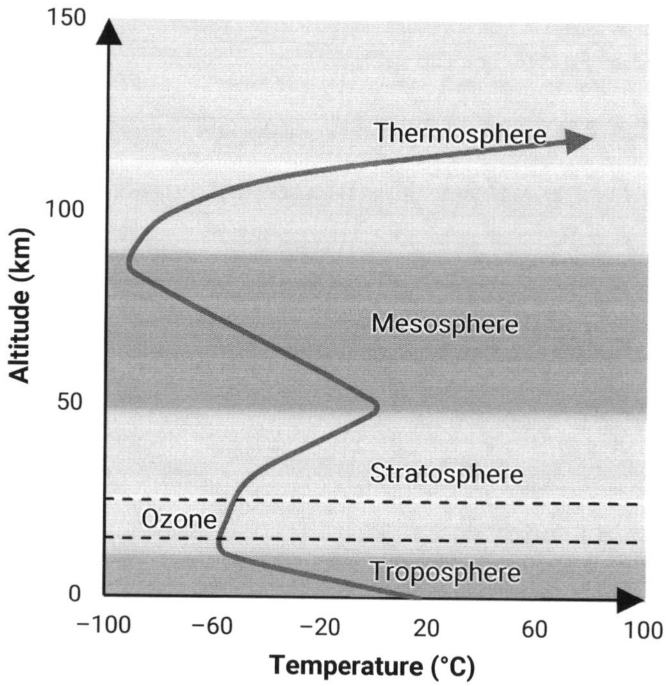

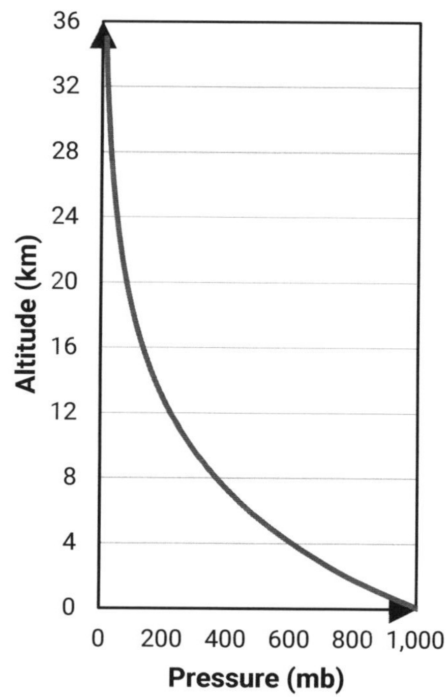

The Earth's atmosphere is comprised of multiple layers with very different temperature characteristics. Closest to the surface, the *troposphere* contains approximately 75 percent of the atmosphere's mass and 99 percent of its water vapor and aerosols. Temperature fluctuations cause constant mixing of air in the troposphere through convection, but it generally becomes cooler as altitude increases.

The *stratosphere* is heated by the absorption of ultraviolet radiation from the sun. Since its lower layers are composed of cooler, heavier air, there is no convective mixing in the stratosphere, and it is quite stable.

The *mesosphere* is the atmospheric layer directly above the stratosphere. Here, temperature decreases as altitude increases due to decreased solar heating and—to a degree—CO_2. In the lower atmosphere, CO_2 acts as a greenhouse gas by absorbing infrared radiation from the Earth's surface. In the mesosphere, CO_2 cools the atmosphere by radiating heat into space.

Above this layer lies the *thermosphere*. At these altitudes, atmospheric gases form layers according to their molecular masses. Temperatures increase with altitude due to absorption of solar radiation by the small amount of residual oxygen. Temperatures are highly dependent on solar activity and can rise to 1,500 °C.

4. The lowest temperatures in the Earth's atmosphere are recorded within the:

a. Troposphere
b. Stratosphere
c. Mesosphere
d. Thermosphere

5. Which of the following would create the greatest amount of genetic variation in a single generation?

a. Crossing over
b. Mutation
c. Hybridization
d. Independent assortment of homologs

6. Which section of the digestive system is responsible for water reabsorption without producing digestive enzymes?

a. The large intestine
b. The duodenum
c. The small intestine
d. The gallbladder

7. Which of the following chemical moieties forms the backbone of DNA?

a. Nitrogenous bases
b. Glycerol
c. Amino groups
d. Pentose and phosphate

8. Molten magnesium chloride is electrolyzed. The products formed from this reaction are:

a. Mg at the anode and Cl^- at the cathode
b. Mg^{2+} at the anode and Cl^- at the cathode
c. Mg at the cathode and Cl_2 at the anode
d. Mg at the anode and Cl_2 at the cathode

9. In birds, gastrulation occurs along the

a. Dorsal lip of the embryo
b. Embryonic disc
c. Primitive streak
d. Circular blastopore

Refer to the following for question 10:

The illustration below depicts the rock cycle. This cycle illustrates the fact that rocks are not unchanging entities; they undergo changes over time.

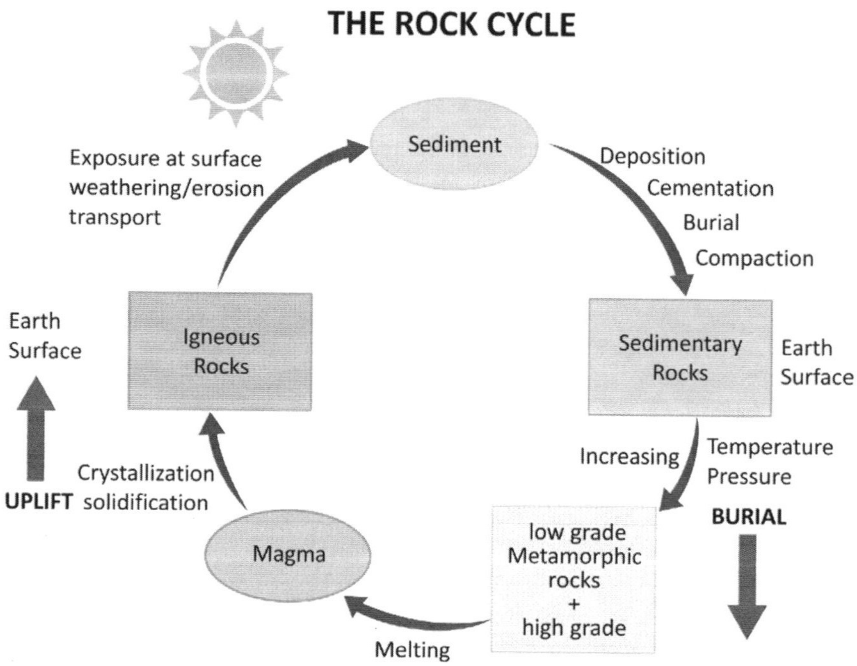

10. How are igneous rocks formed in the rock cycle?

a. Years of sediment are laid down on top of each other and forced together.
b. Acid rain caused by pollution creates holes in metamorphic rocks.
c. Dust and pebbles are pressed together underground from Earth's heat and pressure.
d. Magma from a volcanic eruption cools and hardens.

11. Semiconductors belong to what group of elements?

a. Alkaline earth metals
b. Halogens
c. Metalloids
d. Noble gases

Refer to the following for question 12:

The fossilized remains of a bat have been found in volcanic rock dated to A.D. 79. Scientists studying the bat believe it to be an extinct species.

12. What would be the best way for scientists to confirm that the bat belonged to that particular extinct species?

a. Compare the fossilized remains of this bat with the fossilized remains of other species killed in the eruption.
b. Search for live specimens of the fossilized species.
c. Compare the fossilized remains of this bat with bats known to be from that species.
d. Test the genetic make-up of the fossilized bat.

13. A long nail is heated at one end. After a few seconds, the other end of the nail becomes equally hot. What type of heat transfer does this represent?

a. Radiation
b. Conduction
c. Convection
d. Entropy

14. Which element will most likely form a covalently bonded compound when it bonds with sulfur?

a. Argon (Ar)
b. Iron (Fe)
c. Lithium (Li)
d. Oxygen (O)

15. Which of the following creates a magnetic field?

a. The spinning and rotating of electrons in atoms
b. The separation of charged particles in atoms
c. The vibrational and translational motion of atoms
d. Loosely held valence electrons surrounding an atom

16. Which of the following molecules exhibits ionic bonding?

a. NaCl
b. CO_2
c. $C_6H_{12}O_6$
d. H_2O

17. Which hormone is NOT secreted by the placenta throughout pregnancy?

a. Human chorionic gonadotropin (hCG)
b. Gonadotropin-releasing hormone (GnRH)
c. Estrogen
d. Progesterone

18. Which organisms depend most on light to survive?

a. Undersea plants
b. Mammalians
c. Land plants
d. Humans

19. Which of the following processes is NOT part of the formation of sedimentary rock?

a. Layering
b. Cementation
c. Compaction
d. Heat

20. Which of the following structures is NOT present in gymnosperms?

a. Leaves
b. Pollen
c. Flowers
d. Stomata

21. Which of the following are incorrect Lewis structures?

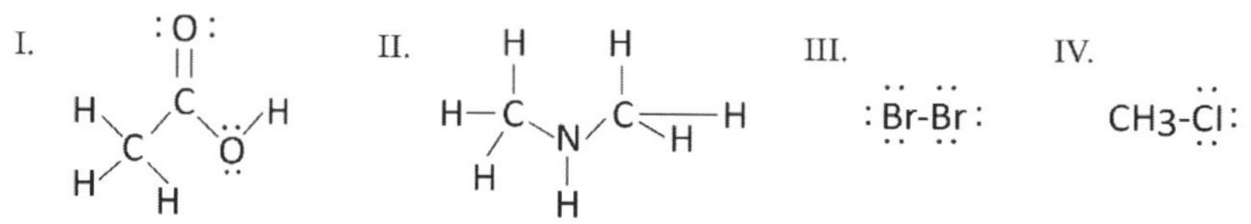

a. I and II
b. II and IV
c. I and III
d. III and IV

22. Cobalt-63 can be produced in a laboratory and is unstable. When it decays, a neutron in its core will likely decay into a proton, changing Cobalt-63 into Nickel-63. Which of the following products will be emitted from this transition?

I. alpha particles
II. beta particle
III. gamma rays

a. I only
b. III only
c. II and III
d. I, II and III

23. Which of the following extraembryonic membranes is an important source of nutrition in many nonhuman animal species but NOT in humans?

a. Amnion
b. Allantois
c. Yolk sac
d. Chorion

24. Which of the following are required by all typical organisms in order to survive?

a. Water, cells, shelter, and space
b. Food, water, cellular growth, nurturing
c. Food, water, sunlight, and air
d. Air, shelter, space, and companionship

25. The electrolysis of water is an example of which of the following?

a. An adiabatic process
b. A chemical change
c. A synthesis reaction
d. Reverse osmosis

26. Which of the following is NOT a result of ozone layer depletion?

a. Higher UV levels reaching the Earth
b. Increased vitamin D synthesis
c. Damage to marine life such as plankton
d. Increased crop yields of wheat, corn, and soybeans

27. Which of the following is NOT a characteristic of enzymes?

a. They change shape when they bind their substrates.
b. They can catalyze reactions in both forward and reverse directions.
c. Their activity is sensitive to changes in temperature.
d. They are always active on more than one kind of substrate.

Refer to the following for question 28:

1 IA	2 IIA	3 IIIB	4 IVB	5 VB	6 VIB	7 VIIB	8	9 VIIIB	10	11 IB	12 IIB	13 IIIA	14 IVA	15 VA	16 VIA	17 VIIA	18 VIIIA
1 **H** 1.01																	2 **He** 4.00
3 **Li** 6.94	4 **Be** 9.01											5 **B** 10.81	6 **C** 12.01	7 **N** 14.01	8 **O** 16.00	9 **F** 19.00	10 **Ne** 20.18
11 **Na** 22.99	12 **Mg** 24.31											13 **Al** 26.98	14 **Si** 28.09	15 **P** 30.97	16 **S** 32.07	17 **Cl** 35.45	18 **Ar** 39.95
19 **K** 39.1	20 **Ca** 40.08	21 **Sc** 44.96	22 **Ti** 47.88	23 **V** 50.94	24 **Cr** 52.00	25 **Mn** 54.94	26 **Fe** 55.85	27 **Co** 58.93	28 **Ni** 58.69	29 **Cu** 63.55	30 **Zn** 65.39	31 **Ga** 69.72	32 **Ge** 72.61	33 **As** 74.92	34 **Se** 78.96	35 **Br** 79.90	36 **Kr** 83.80
37 **Rb** 85.47	38 **Sr** 87.62	39 **Y** 88.91	40 **Zr** 91.22	41 **Nb** 92.91	42 **Mo** 95.94	43 **Tc** (98)	44 **Ru** 101.07	45 **Rh** 102.91	46 **Pd** 106.42	47 **Ag** 107.87	48 **Cd** 112.41	49 **In** 114.82	50 **Sn** 118.71	51 **Sb** 121.76	52 **Te** 127.6	53 **I** 126.9	54 **Xe** 131.29
55 **Cs** 132.9	56 **Ba** 137.3	57 **La*** 138.9	72 **Hf** 178.5	73 **Ta** 180.9	74 **W** 183.9	75 **Re** 186.2	76 **Os** 190.2	77 **Ir** 192.2	78 **Pt** 195.1	79 **Au** 197.0	80 **Hg** 200.6	81 **Tl** 204.4	82 **Pb** 207.2	83 **Bi** 209	84 **Po** (209)	85 **At** (210)	86 **Rn** (222)
87 **Fr** (223)	88 **Ra** (226)	89 **Ac^** (227)	104 **Rf** (261)	105 **Db** (262)	106 **Sg** (263)	107 **Bh** (264)	108 **Hs** (265)	109 **Mt** (268)	110 **Ds** (271)	111 **Rg** (272)							

*	58 **Ce** 140.1	59 **Pr** 140.9	60 **Nd** 144.2	61 **Pm** (145)	62 **Sm** 150.4	63 **Eu** 152.0	64 **Gd** 157.3	65 **Tb** 158.9	66 **Dy** 162.5	67 **Ho** 164.9	68 **Er** 167.3	69 **Tm** 168.9	70 **Yb** 173.0	71 **Lu** 175.0
^	90 **Th** 232.0	91 **Pa** (231)	92 **U** 238.0	93 **Np** (237)	94 **Pu** (244)	95 **Am** (243)	96 **Cm** (247)	97 **Bk** (247)	98 **Cf** (251)	99 **Es** (252)	100 **Fm** (257)	101 **Md** (258)	102 **No** (259)	103 **Lr** (260)

*Note: The row labeled with * is the lanthanide series, and the row labeled with ^ is the actinide series.*

28. On average, how many neutrons does one atom of bromine (Br) have?

a. 35
b. 44.9
c. 45
d. 79.9

29. Which of the following kinds of plants is most likely to perform CAM photosynthesis?

a. Mosses
b. Grasses
c. Deciduous trees
d. Cacti

30. A virus that has been incorporated into the DNA of its host is called a:

a. Lysogenic cycle
b. Lytic cycle
c. Retrovirus
d. Provirus

31. If a population reaches a maximum size and ceases to grow due to a limited availability of resources, which of the following describes the population?

a. Unstable
b. Shrinking exponentially
c. At carrying capacity
d. Moving towards extinction

32. Remoras are fish that attach themselves to sharks and feed on the food particles left over by the larger fish. The shark is neither harmed nor helped by the remora's actions. This type of symbiotic relationship is best described as:

a. Parasitism
b. Commensalism
c. Mutualism
d. Passive transport

33. Which part of the cell is often called the cell "powerhouse" because it provides energy for cellular functions?

a. Nucleus
b. Cell membrane
c. Mitochondria
d. Cytoplasm

34. Burning fossil fuels releases sulfur dioxide and nitrogen dioxide. These pollutants lead to which environmental problem?

a. Denitrification
b. Acid rain
c. Global climate change
d. Ozone depletion

35. Which of the following has a simple life cycle without a metamorphosis?

a. Frog
b. Newt
c. Grasshopper
d. Human being

36. When you walk barefoot on a hot sidewalk, what process is primarily responsible for heat transfer from the sidewalk to your foot?

a. Conduction
b. Convection
c. Radiation
d. None of the above.

37. Which of the following is a solute?

a. Salt in a mixture of salt and pepper
b. Air in a mixture of ash and air
c. Water in a mixture of salt and water
d. Sugar in a mixture of sugar and water

38. How do animals of the phylum Mollusca respire?

a. Through gills
b. Through a trachea
c. Through book lungs
d. Through muscle contraction

39. Which of the following statements about the physical properties of liquids and gases are true?

I. Liquids and gases are both compressible.
II. Liquids flow, but gases do not.
III. Liquids flow and gases are incompressible.
IV. Liquids flow and gases are compressible.
V. Gases flow and liquids are incompressible.

a. I and III
b. II and IV
c. III and V
d. IV and V

40. Balance the following reaction between sulfuric acid and aluminum hydroxide by filling in the correct stoichiometric values for each chemical.

$$\_\,H_2SO_4 + \_\,Al(OH)_3 \rightarrow \_\,Al_2(SO_4)_3 + \_\,H_2O$$

a. 3, 2, 1, 6
b. 2, 3, 1, 3
c. 3, 3, 2, 6
d. 1, 2, 1, 4

41. Water that evaporates from oceans can precipitate over land due to the process of:

a. Transpiration
b. Advection
c. Sublimation
d. Interception

Refer to the following for questions 42–43:

Diagram of a complete, perfect flower

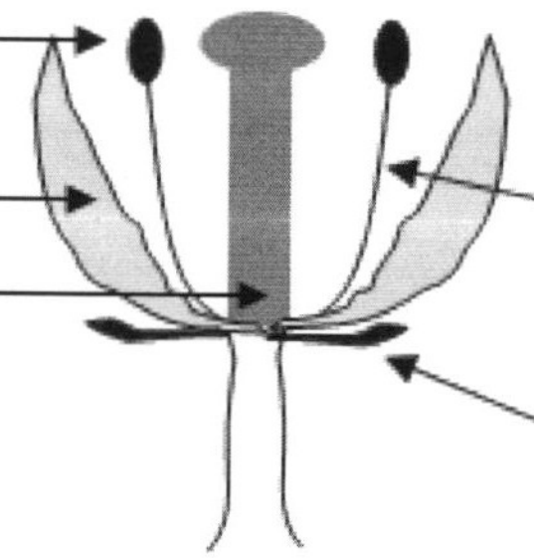

42. The structures composed solely of diploid cells are:

a. 1, 2, and 3
b. 2, 3, and 4
c. 3, 4, and 5
d. 1, 4, and 5

43. The structure in which microspores are produced is:

a. 1
b. 2
c. 3
d. 4

44. Which of the following is a trait that results from disruptive selection?

a. Insecticide resistance
b. Only male peacocks having colorful plumage
c. Some birds having significantly large bills than others within the same species
d. Human height

45. When light passes between different transparent media, its speed is changed by the change in medium and it is refracted, as when a straw in a glass of water seems to break or bend at the waterline. The amount that a medium slows down the speed of light is the:

a. Normal line
b. Wavelength
c. Index of refraction
d. Angle of refraction

46. Which of the following is a disadvantage of biomass energy?

a. Using it releases a lot of carbon.
b. It is non-renewable.
c. It requires a lot of space.
d. Current processes require rare earth metals to utilize the energy.

47. Scientists often form hypotheses based on particular observations. Which of the following is NOT true of a good hypothesis?

a. A good hypothesis is complex.
b. A good hypothesis is testable.
c. A good hypothesis is logical.
d. A good hypothesis predicts future events.

48. Which of the atomic models listed below is the most recent?

a. Rutherford's atomic model
b. Bohr's atomic model
c. Thomson's atomic model
d. Dalton's atomic model

49. Which of the following would most likely be disruptive to the flowering time of a day-neutral plant?

a. Daylight interrupted by a brief dark period
b. Daylight interrupted by a long dark period
c. High daytime temperatures
d. Night interrupted by a brief exposure to red light

50. Which of the following plant structures allows for gas exchange?

a. Xylem
b. Phloem
c. Cuticle
d. Stomata

51. Thermohaline circulation is caused by:

a. Temperature differences between seawater only
b. Salinity differences between seawater only
c. Variations in seawater density caused by both temperature and salinity differences
d. Variations in seawater density caused by extreme wind and storm events

52. In the field of stratigraphy, the relative ages of rocks may be determined by examining which of the following types of evidence?

a. The dates the rocks were formed and the ages of fossils deposited within the rocks
b. Evidence of changes in detrital remanent magnetism when the rock was deposited
c. The vertical layering pattern of the rock
d. All of the above

53. Which set of scientific thinkers is related to the study of chemistry?

a. Newton, Einstein, Feynman, and Hawking
b. Hooke, Pasteur, Watson & Crick, and Jacob & Monod
c. Ibn Hayyan, Lavoisier, Mendeleev, and Curie
d. Hutton, Darwin, Cuvier, and Wegener

54. Which of the following is true about how light interacts with matter?

a. The sky is blue because molecules in the atmosphere scatter short-wavelength (blue) light more than other colors.
b. The sky is blue because the atmosphere absorbs only blue wavelengths.
c. Glass is transparent to all of the frequencies of light within the spectrum.
d. Wood, metal, and other opaque materials reflect all wavelengths of light.

55. Which of the following lists some of the vertebrae in the human skeleton in descending order?

a. Atlas, axis, thoracic, lumbar, sacral, coccyx
b. Axis, sacral, coccyx, atlas, lumbar, thoracic
c. Thoracic, sacral, lumbar, axis, coccyx, atlas
d. Coccyx, lumbar, axis, sacral, thoracic, atlas

56. Which of the following represents an alpha particle?

a. ${}_{-1}^{0}e$
b. ${}_{1}^{2}\mathrm{H}^{+}$
c. ${}_{2}^{4}\mathrm{He}^{2+}$
d. ${}_{+1}^{0}e$

57. The symbol for a calcium ion is Ca^{2+}. Which of the following statements is true concerning this ion?

a. This cation has fewer electrons than protons.
b. This anion has fewer electrons than protons.
c. This cation has more electrons than protons.
d. This anion has more electrons than protons.

58. In an amusement park ride, you stand on the floor of a cylindrical ring with your back touching the wall. The ring begins to rotate, slowly at first, but then faster and faster. When the ring is rotating fast enough, the floor is removed. You do not slide down but remain pressed against the wall of the ring. Which is the best explanation for why you don't fall down?

a. The centripetal force pushes you towards the wall.
b. The centripetal force changes the direction of your motion.
c. The force of friction between the wall and your body is greater than the force of gravity.
d. The rotating ring creates a weightless environment.

59. What is the name for the physical presentation of an organism's genes?

a. Phenotype
b. Species
c. Phylum
d. Genotype

60. Which combination of household chemicals produces a toxic gas?

a. Baking soda and vinegar
b. Bleach and ammonia
c. Water and sugar
d. Vinegar and antacid tablets
e. Rubbing alcohol and table salt

61. According to the Köppen Climate Classification System, regions with continental climates are most commonly found:

a. In the interior regions of large landmasses
b. Near the equator
c. Near the Earth's poles
d. In places with high temperatures year-round

62. The part of the human excretory system most responsible for maintaining normal body temperature is the:

a. kidney.
b. bladder.
c. liver.
d. sweat glands.

63. Which of the following statements regarding chemiosmosis in mitochondria is NOT correct?

a. ATP synthase is powered by protons flowing through membrane channels.
b. Energy from ATP is used to transport protons to the intermembrane space.
c. Energy from the electron transport chain is used to transport protons to the intermembrane space.
d. An electrical gradient and a pH gradient both exist across the inner membrane.

64. Transfer of DNA between bacteria using a narrow tube called a pilus is known as:

a. Transformation
b. Transduction
c. Operation
d. Conjugation

Refer to the following for question 65:

A teacher in Arizona takes her class on a walk through a nearby park to study the flora and fauna of their local desert ecosystem. The students see cacti, snakes, and even evidence of coyote activity.

65. How should the teacher explain to students how these organisms are able to survive in harsh desert conditions?

a. Over thousands of years, these organisms have developed adaptations to survive in arid climates.
b. These organisms migrate out of the desert during the summer months, only living in the desert for a portion of the year.
c. Snakes, cacti, and coyotes work together to find sources of food and water.
d. Snakes, cacti, and coyotes are all aquatic species that live in ponds and rivers during the hot day.

66. Which of the following correctly describes cloud formation?

a. Clouds form when evaporation and condensation are in dynamic equilibrium.
b. Clouds form when there are no condensation nuclei in the air.
c. Clouds form when the atmospheric temperature reaches the dew point.
d. Clouds form when the relative humidity is 0%.

67. Which of the following is a scalar quantity?

a. Acceleration
b. Velocity
c. Speed
d. Force

68. Which of the following statements about galaxies is true?

a. Galaxies are the only structures in the universe that do not contain dark matter.
b. Galaxies are gravitationally bound, meaning structures within the galaxy orbit around its center.
c. Galaxies typically contain over one trillion stars.
d. Galaxies are composed of clusters and superclusters.

69. Which graph segments below represent constant speed?

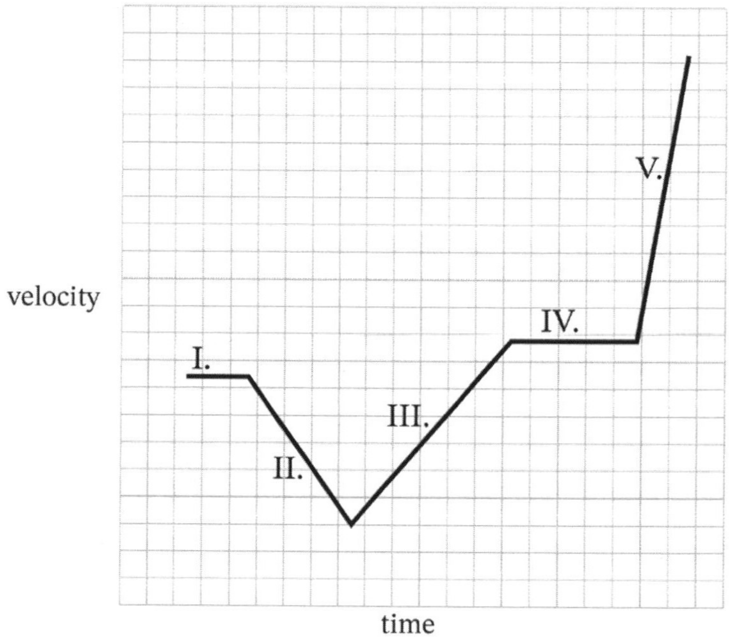

a. I and IV
b. III and V
c. II, III, and V
d. II and III

70. The majority of weather phenomena occur in which part of the Earth's atmosphere?

a. Troposphere
b. Stratosphere
c. Hydrosphere
d. Ionosphere

71. Nora makes soup by adding some spices to a pot of boiling water and stirring the spices until completely dissolved. Next, she adds several chopped vegetables. What is the solute in her mixture?

a. Water
b. Vegetables
c. Spices
d. Heat

72. During primary succession, which species would most likely be a pioneer species?

a. Lichens
b. Fir trees
c. Mosquitoes
d. Dragonflies

73. What property of light explains why a pencil in a glass of water appears to be bent?

a. Reflection
b. Refraction
c. Angle of incidence = angle of reflection
d. Constructive interference

74. Coral reefs are an important ecosystem within the world's oceans. They act as a filtering system, reduce the amount of carbon dioxide in the water, provide shelter for many organisms, and offer economic benefits to many people around the world; however, coral reefs are in danger of being irreversibly destroyed. Which of the following is NOT a cause of the destruction of coral reefs?

a. Reattachment of salvaged coral colonies on the reef
b. Global warming
c. Collection of coral by people to sell
d. Water pollution

75. Hund's rule regarding electronic configuration states:

a. Electrons in the same orbital must have an opposite spin.
b. Electrons must fill lower energy orbitals before filling higher energy orbitals.
c. Electrons must populate empty orbitals of equal energy before filling occupied orbitals.
d. Electrons must have the same nuclear spin as the nucleus.

76. Genetic engineering:

a. Is a form of human reproduction
b. Always involves using restriction enzymes to cut DNA
c. Always involves transient expression of genes
d. Often involves using nucleases to cut DNA

77. Earth's oceans have many little waves that are caused by the various wind speeds around the globe. However, one type of wave is caused by a celestial body. Which celestial body causes this wave?

a. Sun
b. Stars
c. Planets
d. Moon

78. Which answer balances the following equation?

$$CO_2 + H_2O + Energy = C_6H_{12}O_6 + O_2$$

a. $12CO_2 + 6H_2O + Energy = C_6H_{12}O_6 + 6O_2$
b. $6CO_2 + 6H_2O + Energy = 2C_6H_{12}O_6 + 12O_2$
c. $12CO_2 + 6H_2O + Energy = 2C_6H_{12}O_6 + 6O_2$
d. $6CO_2 + 6H_2O + Energy = C_6H_{12}O_6 + 6O_2$

79. Which of the following would not be used as evidence for evolution?

a. Fossil record
b. DNA sequences
c. Anatomical structures
d. Reproductive habits

80. What causes the motion of glaciers?

a. Gravity
b. Erosion
c. Wind
d. Temperature change

81. Which graph segment below represents the greatest acceleration?

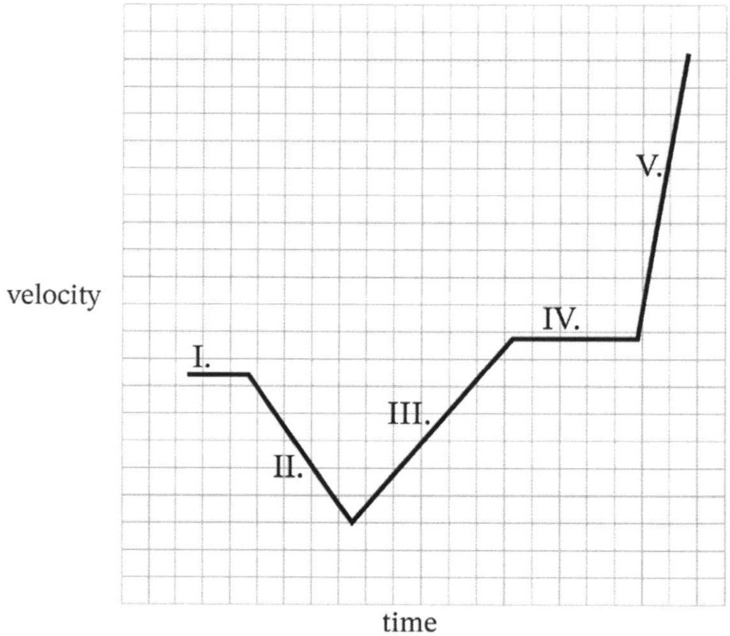

a. II
b. III
c. V
d. III and V

82. A solid is heated until it melts. Which of the following is true about the solid melting?

a. ΔH is positive, and ΔS is positive.
b. ΔH is negative and ΔS is positive.
c. ΔH is positive and ΔS is negative.
d. ΔH is negative and ΔS is negative.

83. Which of the following is a characteristic of a reputable scientific journal?

a. Peer review of the quality of research
b. Famous scientists on the editorial board
c. Use of color graphics to represent data
d. Statistical analysis of all research data

84. To which class of minerals do corundum and magnetite belong?

a. Halides
b. Silicates
c. Native elements
d. Oxides

85. Methylmercury is a toxin produced indirectly from what energy source?

a. Oil
b. Natural gas
c. Wood
d. Coal

86. What happens to a nucleus when it emits an alpha particle?

a. Its atomic number decreases by one.
b. Its mass decreases by two atomic mass units.
c. Its nucleon number decreases by four.
d. Its charge increases by +2.

87. All salts are made from a combination of what two types of substances?

a. A metal and a nonmetal
b. A nonmetal and an alkaline earth metal
c. A cation and an anion
d. A metal and a halogen

88. Which of the following statements about energy is false?

a. Mechanical energy is always conserved in an isolated system.
b. Total energy is always conserved in an isolated system.
c. Energy is never created or destroyed.
d. Matter can be transformed into energy

89. The frequency of ocean waves is measured by:

a. The vertical distance between a wave's crest and trough
b. The horizontal distance between the crests of two subsequent waves
c. The time between two subsequent wave crests
d. The number of wave crests that pass a given point each second

90. Which of the following is an example of a chemical change?

a. Salt dissolving in water
b. Water evaporating
c. Silver tarnishing
d. Dry ice sublimating

91. Which of the following numbers has 4 significant figures?

a. 3,020.5
b. 0.003020
c. 3.2005
d. 0.0325

92. All of the following are true regarding wind energy, EXCEPT:

a. Wind turbines use space inefficiently, but they have low operational costs.
b. Wind is not a reliable source of energy in all geographic locations.
c. Wind turbines are expensive to manufacture and install.
d. Wind turbines are a threat to wildlife.

93. When using a microscope, which objective provides the greatest field of view?

a. 4X
b. 10X
c. 40X
d. 100X

94. Which of the following divisions of plants produces seeds for reproduction?

a. Anthophyta
b. Lycophyta
c. Sphenophyta
d. Pterophyta

95. Which of the following equations for sound waves correctly relates frequency to wavelength and speed of sound?

a. $f \times \lambda = v$
b. $f = \lambda \times v$
c. $f = \lambda + v$
d. $f \times \lambda \times v = 1$

96. Which of the following apparent colors of stars indicates the coolest temperature?

a. Orange red
b. Yellow orange
c. Yellow white
d. Blue white

97. Which of the following correctly lists the periods that make up the Mesozoic era, from earliest to most recent?

a. Jurassic, Triassic, Cretaceous
b. Permian, Triassic, Jurassic
c. Triassic, Jurassic, Cretaceous
d. Triassic, Jurassic, Permian

98. If an astronomer observing the stars detects a blue shift, what could he conclude?

a. The star is moving farther away from him.
b. The star is moving closer or toward him.
c. The star is cooling down and becoming smaller.
d. The star is heating up and becoming larger.

99. In an ecosystem, its abiotic factors:

a. Are alive.
b. Are not alive.
c. Do not affect living organisms.
d. Include some microorganisms.

100. The best way to separate isotopes of the same element is to exploit:

a. Differences in chemical reactivity
b. Differences in reduction potential
c. Differences in toxicity
d. Differences in mass

101. When an animal takes in more energy than it uses over an extended time, the extra chemical energy is stored as:

a. Fat
b. Starch
c. Protein
d. Enzymes

102. According to the laboratory safety rules, what should students be instructed to do first in case of a laboratory fire?

a. Notify the instructor
b. Locate the nearest exit
c. Use the fire extinguisher
d. Open the windows

103. How are lipids different from other organic molecules?

a. They consist of repeating monomers to form long chains.
b. They are not water soluble.
c. They serve as catalysts.
d. Lipids store less energy per gram than carbohydrates or proteins.

104. For electricity to flow and move, it requires which of these?

a. A generator and an insulator
b. A generator and a conductor
c. A conductor and an insulator
d. Electricity needs all of these.

105. Which of the following types of rock solidifies deepest beneath the Earth's surface?

a. Hypabyssal
b. Plutonic
c. Volcanic
d. Detrital

106. Which of the following is NOT a correct representation of the average salinity of seawater?

a. 35 parts per thousand
b. 3.5 parts per hundred
c. 3.5%
d. 35%

107. A spoon that is placed in a bowl of hot soup becomes warm as a result of:

a. Convection
b. Conduction
c. Radiation
d. Advection

108. Of the following actions, which best represents the science process skill of Inference?

a. Formulating new hypotheses based on experimental results
b. Finding patterns and meaning in the results of experiments
c. Identifying properties of things/situations using the senses
d. Reporting experimental results and conclusions to others

109. Which type of nuclear process features atomic nuclei splitting apart to form smaller nuclei?

a. Fission
b. Fusion
c. Decay
d. Ionization

110. The Earth's magnetic field protects it from:

a. Excess heat from the Sun
b. Radio waves from black holes
c. Solar wind
d. Impacts from space debris

111. The Cretaceous-Tertiary event, during which non-avian dinosaurs became extinct, occurred approximately how long ago?

a. 10,000 years ago
b. 15.5 million years ago
c. 38 million years ago
d. 65.5 million years ago

112. Which of the following statements best describes the physical structure of the universe?

a. Galaxies are the largest structures in the universe, and they are distributed evenly throughout space.
b. Superclusters are the largest structures in the universe, and they are distributed evenly throughout space.
c. Superclusters are the largest structures in the universe, and they are unevenly distributed so that large voids exist in space.
d. Filaments are the largest structures in the universe, and they surround large, bubble-like voids.

113. Which of the following general statements concerning ideal gases is true?

a. Volume is inversely proportional to kinetic energy.
b. Volume is inversely proportional to number of moles.
c. Volume is inversely proportional to temperature.
d. Volume is inversely proportional to pressure.

114. Pollination involves which plant parts?

a. Xylem and petiole
b. Apical meristem and floral meristem
c. Anther and stigma
d. Root hairs and stroma

115. Which of the following materials has randomly aligned dipoles?

a. A non-magnetic substance
b. An electromagnet
c. A permanent magnet
d. A horseshoe magnet

116. The Coriolis effect in the Earth's oceans is caused by:

a. The Earth's rotation
b. The Earth's magnetic field
c. Variations in the density of seawater
d. The Gulf Stream

117. The following is the anticodon sequence formed during translation. What is the mRNA codon sequence?

A C G U A C G C U

a. T G C A T G C G A
b. U G C T U G C G T
c. U G C A U G C G A
d. U C G A U C G C A

118. Which of the following is NOT a factor as to why lakes don't freeze solid in winter?

a. Water has its lowest volume at zero degrees Celsius.
b. As water freezes, the ice floats due to its lower density than the surrounding water.
c. Due to hydrogen bonding, ice forms six-sided crystals that have a larger volume than six water molecules.
d. The water exposed to the cold air freezes first, forming a good insulator between the air and the water beneath it.

119. Which of the following are formed when the plasma membrane surrounds a particle outside of the cell?

a. Golgi bodies
b. Rough endoplasmic reticulum
c. Secretory vesicles
d. Endocytic vesicles

120. When a solid is heated and transforms directly into the gaseous phases, this process is called:

a. Sublimation
b. Fusion
c. Diffusion
d. Condensation

121. Isotopes are two atoms of the same element that have different ____. They have the same number of ____, but a different number of ____.

a. mass; protons; neutrons.
b. ionization number; protons; electrons.
c. charge; protons; electrons.
d. mass; protons; electrons.

122. Which of the following is true of the gastrula?

a. It is a solid ball of cells.
b. It has three germ layers.
c. It is an extraembryonic membrane.
d. It gives rise to the blastula.

123. Which of the following is true concerning the benefits of radiation therapy?

a. Radiation therapy cannot be used to reduce pain.
b. Radiation therapy is given only to shrink tumors.
c. Radiation therapy kills only cancer cells.
d. Radiation therapy kills cancer cells by damaging their DNA.

124. An inch is approximately equivalent to which of the following?

a. 25.4 mm
b. 25.4 cm
c. 2.54×10^{-4} km
d. 2.54×10^{2} m

125. How does meiosis differ from mitosis?

a. Meiosis is used to repair the body. Mitosis is used to break down the body.
b. Meiosis is used for asexual reproduction of single-celled organisms. Mitosis is used for sexual reproduction of multicellular organisms.
c. Meiosis only occurs in humans. Mitosis only occurs in plants.
d. Meiosis produces cells that are genetically different. Mitosis produces cells that are genetically identical.

126. Chemical compounds are formed when:

a. Valence electrons from atoms of two different elements are shared or transferred.
b. Valence electrons from multiple atoms of a single element are shared or transferred.
c. The nuclei of two atoms are joined together.
d. The nucleus of an atom is split.

127. In insects whose life cycles include an incomplete metamorphosis, which stage of the metamorphosis does not take place?

a. The egg
b. The larva
c. The imago
d. The pupa

128. Which of the following is not an advantage angiosperms show over other types of plants?

a. Larger leaves
b. Double fertilization
c. Dormant seeds
d. Lower seed dispersal

129. Which of the following is a source of renewable energy?

a. Nuclear power
b. Natural gas
c. Geothermal power
d. Crude oil

130. What is the best use for a barometer?

a. Measuring temperature
b. Measuring atmospheric pressure
c. Observing remote objects
d. Viewing objects too small for the naked eye to see

131. All of the following are common ways of controlling eukaryotic gene expression EXCEPT:

a. Regulatory proteins
b. Nucleosome packing
c. Methylation of DNA
d. Operons

132. Graham's law is best used to determine what relationship between two different materials?

a. Pressure and volume
b. Volume and temperature
c. Mass and diffusion rate
d. Diffusion rate and temperature

133. Newton's First law of motion states that:

a. An object at rest tends to stay at rest unless an opposing force changes this.
b. An object stays at rest or in motion unless/until an opposing force changes it.
c. An object in motion tends to stay in motion until an opposing force changes it.
d. For every action that take place, there is an equal and opposite reaction to it.

134. According to Kepler's laws of planetary motion, which of the following statements is true?

a. The planets orbit the Sun in circular paths.
b. A vector from the Sun to a planet sweeps out equal areas in equal times.
c. Planets located further from the Sun have shorter periods than planets located nearer to the Sun.
d. While orbiting the Sun, the closer the planet is to the Sun, the slower it travels.

Refer to the following for question 135:

Diagram representing a cross section of a tree trunk:

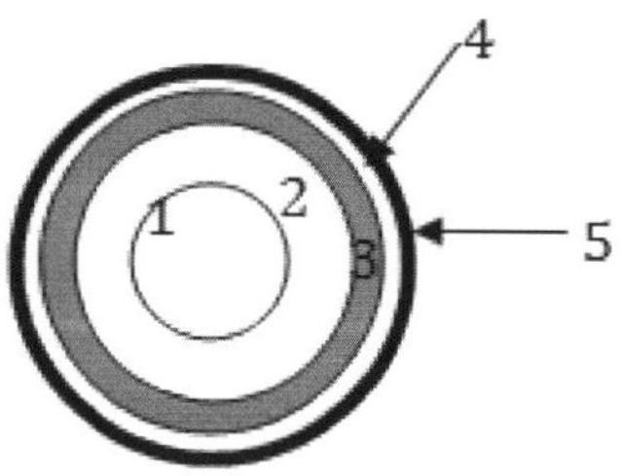

135. Which structure transports carbohydrates to the roots?

a. 1
b. 2
c. 3
d. 4

136. Tropical climate zones are characterized by:

a. Extreme temperature variations between night and day
b. Extreme temperature variations between seasons
c. Frequent rainfall
d. All of the above

137. Which color of light has the highest frequency?

a. Blue
b. Red
c. Green
d. Violet

138. Which of the following statements about radioactive decay is true?

a. The sum of the mass of the daughter particles is less than that of the parent nucleus.
b. The sum of the mass of the daughter particles is greater than that of the parent nucleus.
c. The sum of the mass of the daughter particles is equal to that of the parent nucleus.
d. The sum of the mass of the daughter particles cannot be accurately measured.

139. Which of the following is NOT a product of respiration?

a. Carbon dioxide
b. Water
c. Glucose
d. ATP

140. Which of the following correctly describes the image of a double concave lens?

a. Reduced, upright, virtual image
b. Enlarged, upright, virtual image
c. Reduced, inverted, virtual image
d. Reduced, upright, real image

141. When working in the laboratory, what is the minimum length of time an eye should be flushed if a chemical gets in the eye?

a. 2 minutes
b. 10 minutes
c. 15 minutes
d. 30 minutes

142. When the accumulation of snow and ice exceeds ablation, which of the following occurs as a direct result?

a. An iceberg breaks free from a glacier.
b. A glacier gradually forms.
c. A glacier slowly erodes.
d. A lake forms within a glacier.

143. One mole of oxygen gas and two moles of hydrogen are combined in a sealed container at STP. Which of the following statements is true?

a. The mass of hydrogen gas is greater than the mass of oxygen.
b. The volume of hydrogen is greater than the volume of oxygen.
c. The hydrogen and oxygen will react to produce two moles of water.
d. The partial pressure of hydrogen is greater than the partial pressure of oxygen.

144. What is the name of the process by which plants generate their own food source using sunlight, carbon dioxide, and water?

a. Photoemission
b. Chemotherapy
c. Chemosynthesis
d. Photosynthesis

145. How many electrons are in an uncharged atom of $^{45}_{20}Ca$?

a. 20
b. 45
c. 65
d. 25

146. According to Newton's law of universal gravitation, what happens to the force of attraction between two objects if the distance between them is doubled?

a. The force is reduced to one-half of the original amount.
b. The force is reduced to one-fourth of the original amount.
c. The force is quadrupled.
d. The force is doubled.

147. When a population reaches its carrying capacity:

a. Other populations will be forced out of the habitat.
b. Density-dependent factors no longer play a role.
c. Density-independent factors no longer play a role.
d. The population growth rate approaches zero.

148. Which of the following statements regarding the principle of uniformitarianism is true?

a. Uniformitarianism is an argument for catastrophism.
b. Uniformitarianism is a key building block for Darwin's theory of evolution.
c. Uniformitarianism states that the past is the key to the present.
d. Uniformitarianism states that the fittest organisms will survive to reproduce.

149. Evidence of a chemical reaction can be determined by all of the following EXCEPT:

a. A modification in the arrangement of atoms
b. An endothermic or exothermic reaction
c. The formation of a gas
d. There being no change in energy

150. Plant A undergoes C4 photosynthesis. What type of environment would the plant most likely live in?

a. Plant A lives in a very cold environment.
b. Plant A lives in a very hot environment.
c. Plant A lives in a marine environment.
d. Plant A lives in a dark environment that lacks solar energy.

151. The main function of ______ is to reduce the number of chromosomes to half the number of parent cells.

a. mitosis
b. telophase
c. meiosis I
d. meiosis II

152. What type of chemical bond connects the oxygen and hydrogen atoms in a molecule of water?

a. Static bond
b. Aquatic bond
c. Ionic bond
d. Covalent bond

153. What is 119 K in degrees Celsius?

a. 32 °C
b. −154 °C
c. 154 °C
d. −32 °C

154. Metamorphic rock is produced when which of the following undergoes profound changes as a result of exposure to intense pressure and heat?

a. A batholith
b. A protolith
c. An igneous rock
d. A sedimentary rock

155. Once a hypothesis has been verified and accepted, it becomes which of the following?

a. A fact
b. A law
c. A conclusion
d. A theory

156. Which of the following does NOT display an appropriate or safe use of chemicals?

a. Never taste any chemicals.
b. To test odors, waft the odors towards your nose with a cupped hand.
c. Never return unused chemicals to the stock bottle.
d. When diluting acids, always pour the water into the acid.

157. Which of the following statements is NOT true about the period of a simple pendulum?

a. As the mass of a pendulum increases, the period increases.
b. For small amplitudes, the period of a pendulum is approximately independent of amplitude.
c. A pendulum swings more slowly at higher elevation.
d. To double the period of a pendulum, the length must be quadrupled.

158. A pulley lifts a 10-kg object 10 m into the air in 5 minutes. Using this information, you can calculate which of the following?

a. Mechanical advantage
b. Efficiency
c. Frictional resistance
d. Power

159. According to the Dana classification system, gold, silver, and copper belong to which class?

a. Organic
b. Elemental
c. Oxide
d. Sulfide

160. Nuclear chain reactions, such as the kind that is exploited in nuclear power plants, are propagated by what subatomic particle(s)?

a. Protons
b. Neutrons
c. Electrons
d. Neutrons and protons

Answer Key and Explanations for Test #1

1. B: The shaking that is observed during an earthquake is a direct result of seismic waves. Seismic waves are vibrations that travel through earth when rock slippage along a fault occurs. There are two types of seismic waves: body waves and surface waves. Body waves can either be primary, or P waves, and secondary, or S waves. P waves move more quickly than S waves and create motion that radiates directly outward from the point of origin. S waves produce a shearing, or side-to-side, motion. The other type of seismic wave is a surface wave, which causes much of the shaking felt at Earth's surface.

2. B: Glass cleaner traditionally was a 5% ammonia solution. Recently most glass cleaners are more environmentally friendly solutions containing much less ammonia. Bleach is a solution of 3-6% sodium hypochlorite.

3. B: Making a determination based on the results of a controlled experiment is a description of concluding. Inferring can be described as explaining or interpreting observations. Reading an instrument during an experiment is one type of quantitative observation. Comparing includes noting similarities and differences.

4. C: This can be read from the graph. The mesosphere has the coldest temperatures in the atmospheric regions beneath outer space. Beyond the upper limits of the mesosphere, the thermosphere gets progressively hotter. However, it is worth noting that even though the temperature gets really high, the density of molecules and atoms is so low that it would not feel very hot.

5. C: Hybridization produces the greatest genetic variation in a single generation because it combines alleles from genetically distinct individuals or populations, introducing many new allele combinations at once. In contrast, crossing over and independent assortment only reshuffle existing alleles, and mutation introduces new variation more slowly, typically affecting only one or a few genes at a time.

6. A: The large intestine's main function is the reabsorption of water into the body to form solid waste. It also allows for the absorption of vitamin K produced by microbes living inside the large intestine. Unlike the small intestine, which also reabsorbs water, the large intestine does not produce any digestive enzymes.

7. D: DNA is composed of nucleotides joined together in long chains. Nucleotides are composed of a pentose sugar, a phosphate group, and a nitrogenous base. The bases form the "rungs" of the ladder at the core of the DNA helix, and the pentose-phosphates are on its outside, or backbone.

8. C: Reduction takes place at the cathode and oxidation takes place at the anode. Mg^{2+} of the salt will be reduced to Mg at the cathode, and Cl^- will be oxidized to Cl_2 at the anode.

9. C: In birds, the invagination of gastrulation occurs along a line called the primitive streak. Cells migrate to the primitive streak, and the embryo becomes elongated.

10. D: Igneous rocks are formed when magma in the Earth erupts through cracks in the crust. There, the lava cools, creating a hard structure with many air pockets or holes.

11. C: Metalloids have some properties of metals and some properties of nonmetals. Good semiconductors have the properties of metals and nonmetals, providing moderate electrical conductivity that can be regulated through temperature changes and doping.

12. C: To determine if this bat is from a particular species, the remains must be compared with the remains of the other members of the species.

13. B: A long nail or other type of metal, substance, or matter that is heated at one end and then the other end becomes equally hot is an example of conduction. Conduction is energy transfer by neighboring molecules from an area of hotter temperature to cooler temperature. Radiation (A), or thermal radiation, refers to heat being transferred through empty space by electromagnetic radiation. An example is sunlight heating the earth. Convection (C) refers to heat being transferred by molecules moving from one location in the substance to another creating a heat current, usually in a gas or a liquid. Entropy (D) relates to the second law of thermodynamics and refers to how much heat or energy is no longer available to do work in a system. It can also be stated as the amount of disorder in a system.

14. D: Covalent bonds form when two nonmetals bond. Oxygen (O) is the only nonmetal in the answer choices. Iron (Fe) is a transition metal. Lithium (Li) is an alkali metal. Argon (Ar) is a noble gas and does not react with other elements.

15. A: A magnetic field is created by a spin magnetic dipole moment and the orbital magnetic dipole moment of the electrons in atoms. Therefore, it is the spinning and rotating of electrons in atoms that creates a magnetic field. The separation of charged particles in atoms describes the nucleus and electron clouds within an atom. The vibrational and translational motion of atoms creates thermal energy. Loosely held valence electrons surrounding an atom indicates a good electrical conductor.

16. A: Sodium chloride exhibits ionic bonding due to the attraction between Na^+ ions and Cl^- ions. Typically, elements on the opposite sides of the periodic table (a metal and a nonmetal) form ionic bonds. Carbon dioxide, water, and glucose exhibit covalent bonding. Typically, elements on the same side of the periodic table (two or more nonmetals) form covalent bonds.

17. B: The placenta secretes progesterone and estrogen once a pregnancy is established. The placenta secretes hCG early in pregnancy and in small doses throughout the pregnancy.

18. C: Plants growing on land depend on sunlight to perform photosynthesis, the process whereby they convert sunlight's energy to chemical energy as fuel for their life functions. Undersea plants (A) need water and nutrients like land plants; they do not need all gases in the atmosphere but need the gases in the water, and they need less light than land plants, or no light at all, to survive. Mammals (B) need air, water, and nutrients; some mammals need more or less light, but none need light for photosynthesis as land plants do. Humans (D) are also mammals.

19. D: The formation of sedimentary rock does not include heat. Of the three types of rock—igneous, sedimentary, and metamorphic—heat is essential to two: igneous and metamorphic. Sedimentary rocks are formed by sediments that get deposited and then compacted or cemented together. Sedimentary rocks are classified into detrital, organic, or chemical sediments. Answer A, layering, is correct since sediments can be deposited or otherwise formed in layers. Answer B, cementation, is also called lithification. Answer C, compaction, refers to the pressure forming sedimentary rock leading to cementation.

20. C: Gymnosperms reproduce by producing pollen and ovules, but they do not have flowers. Instead, their reproductive structures are cones or cone-like structures.

21. B: The nitrogen is missing its lone pair of electrons, and should have two dots above it. A correct Lewis structure shows how the atoms are connected to each other as well as all of the valence electrons in the compound, so the abbreviated methyl group is also incorrect.

22. C: Cobalt-63 has too many neutrons to be stable. By emitting a beta particle (aka an electron, one of the neutrons in the cobalt is converted to a proton, thereby maintaining the mass number but changing the atomic number from 27 (cobalt) to 28 (nickel). In addition, some energy is radiated away in the form of gamma radiation. Electron emission is usually associated with the emission of gamma rays because the daughter nucleus is not likely to be in a ground state. The daughter nucleus, in other words, is likely to be unstable and emit a gamma ray.

23. C: In birds and reptiles, the yolk sac contains the yolk, the main source of nutrients for the embryo. In humans, the yolk sac is empty and embryos receive nutrition through the placenta. However, the yolk sac forms part of the digestive system and is where the earliest blood cells and blood vessels are formed.

24. C: All typical living organisms need food, water, sunlight, and air. Shelter, space, and nurturing are essential for most organisms, but they are technically indirect needs that are not crucial to sustaining life.

25. B: The electrolysis of water is a chemical change that transforms water into hydrogen and oxygen gases. Synthesis reactions are those that combine reactants to form a product, which is the opposite of what happens when electrolyzing water. Reverse osmosis is a technique often used to purify water by forcing impure water through a semipermeable membrane using a pressure differential.

26. D: Ozone layer depletion results in higher UV levels reaching the earth. These higher levels of UV rays may result in more skin cancer, sunburn, and premature aging of skin, damage to marine life such as plankton, and decreased crop yields of wheat, corn, and soybeans. However, the higher concentration of UV light has increased the amount of vitamin D synthesized in humans.

27. D: Enzymes are substrate-specific. Most enzymes catalyze only one biochemical reaction. Their active sites are specific for a certain type of substrate and do not bind to other substrates and catalyze other reactions.

28. B: To determine the average number of neutrons in one atom of an element, subtract the atomic number from the average atomic mass. For bromine (Br), subtract its atomic number (35) from its average atomic mass (79.9) to acquire the average number of neutrons, 44.9.

29. D: Crassulacean acid metabolism (CAM) photosynthesis occurs in plants that grow where water loss must be minimized, such as cacti. These plants open their stomata and fix CO_2 at night. During the day, stomata are closed, reducing water loss. Thus, photosynthesis can proceed without water loss.

30. D: In the lysogenic cycle, viral DNA gets incorporated into the DNA of the host. A virus in this dormant stage is called a provirus. Eventually, an external cue may trigger the virus to excise itself and begin the lytic cycle.

31. C: A population that reaches maximum size and ceases to grow due to a limited availability of resources is said to be at carrying capacity. The carrying capacity of a species is influenced by many factors such as the amount of land or water available, food supply, and predators. Unstable and moving towards extinction are not correct as carrying capacity does not necessarily mean it is unstable or becoming extinct. Shrinking exponentially is also incorrect as the question says it has stopped growing, not that it is reducing in size.

32. B: Commensalism is a relationship between two organisms in which one organism is benefited and the other is neither harmed nor helped. Parasitism is a relationship in which one organism benefits but the other is harmed. Mutualism is a relationship in which both organisms benefit. Passive transport is a process such as osmosis by which materials are absorbed into cells.

33. C: Mitochondria are often called the power house of the cell because they provide energy for the cell to function. The nucleus is the control center for the cell. The cell membrane surrounds the cell and separates the cell from its environment. Cytoplasm is the thick fluid within the cell membrane that surrounds the nucleus and contains organelles.

34. B: When sulfur dioxide and nitrogen dioxide mix with water and other substances in the atmosphere, they produce sulfuric acid and nitric acid. These acids kill plants and animals when they reach the surface of the earth.

35. D: Human beings, like other mammals, birds, fish, reptiles, and spiders, have simple life cycles in that they are either born live or hatched from eggs, and then grow to adulthood. Frogs (A), newts (B), and grasshoppers (C) undergo metamorphoses wherein their forms change. Frogs and newts are amphibians; they begin life underwater, breathing through gills, but breathe through lungs by adulthood and move from the water to live on the land. Grasshoppers hatch from eggs into larvae, wormlike juvenile forms that do most of the feeding they need; then they progress to adulthood.

36. A: Heat between objects in contact with each other is transferred by conduction, choice A. Convection is transfer by currents within a body of fluid, and radiation is the transfer of heat between objects *not* in contact, through light rays emitted by the hotter object and absorbed by the cooler one.

37. D: In a homogeneous solution, the substance that is dissolved is the solute. A mixture of sugar and water is a homogenous solution in which the sugar is the solute, and the water is the solvent. A mixture of salt and water is a homogeneous solution in which the salt is the solute, and the water is the solvent. A mixture of ash in air is a description of smoke, which is a colloid. A mixture of salt and pepper is a heterogeneous mixture.

38. A: Animals of the phylum Mollusca or mollusks, respire (breathe) through gills. Respiration is the process of taking in oxygen and releasing carbon dioxide. Mollusca consists of several classes that include species as diverse as chitons, clams, land and marine snails, and squid. This represents a diverse range of body structures. Many mollusks have a mantle that includes a cavity that is used for both breathing and excretion. Within the mantle are gills (ctenidia). Mollusks do not have tracheas. Some land snails have a respiratory cavity that is often called a lung but is not a true lung. Spiders, which are not mollusks (they are arachnids), have a type of lungs called book lungs. Muscle contraction is not required for the gills to function. Other structures, such as cilia, work to pass water over the gills.

39. D: Both liquids and gases are fluids and therefore flow, but only gases are compressible. The molecules that make up a gas are very far apart, allowing the gas to be compressed into a smaller volume.

40. A: By comparing the products to the reactants, there must be at least two Al atoms in the starting material, and at least three sulfate groups. Therefore, a coefficient of 2 must be placed in front of $Al(OH)_3$ and a coefficient of 3 must be placed in front of H_2SO_4. To make the number of hydrogen and oxygen atoms equal on both sides of the equation, a coefficient of 6 must be placed in front of H_2O.

41. B: Water that evaporates from oceans can precipitate over land due to advection. Advection is the horizontal movement of air masses by wind. Moist air over the ocean is transported horizontally over land; as this air rises and cools (often by convection or lifting over terrain or fronts), the water vapor condenses and can precipitate over land masses.

42. C: In flowering plants, the anthers house the male gametophytes (which produce sperm) and the pistils house the female gametophytes (which produce eggs). Eggs and sperm are haploid. All other tissues are solely diploid.

43. B: Anthers contain microspore mother cells that undergo meiosis to produce microspores. Each microspore then undergoes mitosis to develop into a pollen grain, which is the male gametophyte of flowering plants.

44. C: Disruptive selection occurs when the environment favors alleles for extreme traits. In the example, seasonal changes can make different types of food available at different times of the year, favoring the large or small bills.

45. C: The amount that a transparent medium slows down the speed of light through it is called the index of refraction. The normal line (A) is an imaginary line that runs at a right angle to the surface of a medium; in the example given, it would be the waterline in the glass of water. The wavelength (B) of the light becomes shorter in proportion to how much the speed of light is slowed by the medium (but the medium does not change the frequency of the light wave, which is a property of the light source). The angle of refraction (D) is the degree to which the light wave is bent by the medium. As an example of refraction indices, diamonds trap light and slow its speed more than water because they are much denser and harder than water; thus, they sparkle more than water does and have a higher index of refraction than water.

46. C: Advantages of biomass energy include that it's renewable, carbon neutral, and abundant. A disadvantage of biomass energy include that it requires space and may be inefficient.

47. A: A good hypothesis is testable and logical, and can be used to predict future events. A good hypothesis is also simple, not complex.

48. B: Dalton stated that atoms are hard spheres. Thomson proposed the plum pudding model, in which electrons are embedded in a sphere of positive charge. Rutherford introduced the planetary model, in which electrons circularly orbit a small central nucleus. Bohr's model stated that electrons move in regions of space called orbits. This would later be expanded to "orbitals" of the later quantum-mechanical model.

49. C: Day-neutral plants are not affected by day length in their flowering times. Rather, they respond to other environmental cues, like temperature and water.

50. D: Stomata are openings on leaves that allow for gas exchange, which is essential for photosynthesis. Stomata are surrounded by guard cells, which open and close based on their turgidity.

51. C: Thermohaline circulation is caused by variations in seawater density caused by both temperature and salinity differences. This process, which affects subsurface ocean currents, contributes to the mixing of seawater and accounts for the relative uniformity of the water's physical and chemical properties.

52. D: The field of stratigraphy is divided into several subfields, each of which focuses on a unique aspect of sedimentary material and yields unique insights about the material's age. In the subfield of chronostratigraphy, a material's age is estimated by determining when it was formed or deposited. The study of the vertical layering of rock types is called lithostratigraphy, and the study of fossil ages in rock layers is called biostratigraphy. Magnetostratigraphy examines data about changes in detrital remanent magnetism (DRM) at the time rocks were formed.

53. C: Jabir Ibn Hayyan, Antoine Lavoisier, Dmitri Mendeleev, and Marie Curie are associated with the study of chemistry. Isaac Newton, Albert Einstein, Richard Feynman, and Stephen Hawking are associated with the study of physics. Robert Hooke, Louis Pasteur, James Watson & Francis Crick, and François Jacob & Jacques Monod are associated with the study of biology. James Hutton, Charles Darwin, Georges Cuvier, and Alfred Wegener are associated with the study of geology.

54. A: The sky looks blue because of Rayleigh scattering, in which air molecules scatter short-wavelength light, especially blue, much more than longer wavelengths. This scattered blue light reaches our eyes from all directions, making the sky look blue. Therefore (B) is incorrect. Glass appears transparent to us; however, it is really only transparent to the light frequencies (wavelengths) that we can see, but to ultraviolet light frequencies, which we cannot see, glass is actually opaque. Wood, metal, and other materials look opaque to us *not* because they reflect light (D) but rather because they absorb light.

55. A: From highest to lowest: the atlas is cervical vertebra 1, supporting the skull; the axis is cervical vertebra 2; next come cervical vertebrae 3 through 7, the bones in the back of the neck, which are omitted in all choices; then, the 12 thoracic vertebrae are the upper back bones; below these are the 5 lumbar vertebrae in the lower back; the 5 sacral vertebrae (together, the sacrum) are the pelvic and hip-level back bones; and the coccyx or tailbone at the bottom of the spine contains 3-5 small bones, which are often fused together.

56. C: Alpha particles are identical to helium nuclei and may be represented as He^{2+}, ${}^4_2He$, or ${}^4_2He^{2+}$. They may also be represented by the Greek letter alpha as α, α^{2+} or ${}^4_2\alpha^{2+}$. Beta particles are high-speed electrons or positrons and are designated by the Greek letter beta as β^- and β^+ or ${}^{0}_{-1}e$ and ${}^{0}_{+1}e$, respectively.

57. A: Cations are positively charged ions. Anions are negatively charged ions; therefore, the ion Ca^{2+} is a cation. Cations are positively charged because they have lost one or more electrons. This cation has lost two electrons and has fewer electrons than protons.

58. C: As the ring spins, the wall of the ring exerts centripetal force on your body. This force also causes friction between your back and the wall, and that's why you don't fall when the floor is removed, assuming the frictional force is large enough to overcome gravity. As the speed of rotation increases, the force exerted by the wall on your body increases, so the frictional force between you and the wall increases. Answer B is factually correct, but it does not explain why you do not fall—centripetal force does cause you to change direction. Also note that "centrifugal force" is an illusion; because you feel the wall pushing against your back, you feel like you're being pushed outwards. In fact, you're being pulled inwards, but the wall is also being pulled inwards and is pushing against you. Finally, choice D is incorrect because you are not weightless on a ride like this.

59. A: *Phenotype* is the physical presentation of an organism's genes. In other words, the phenotype is the physical characteristics of the organism. Phenotype is often contrasted with *genotype*, the genetic makeup of an organism. The genotype of the organism is not visible in its presentation, although some of the characteristics encoded in the genes have to do with physical presentation. A *phylum* is a group of classes that are closely related. A *species* is a group of like organisms that are capable of breeding together and producing similar offspring.

60. B: When combined, bleach and ammonia can release chlorine gas under certain conditions. Baking soda and vinegar (A) release carbon dioxide gas bubbles. Sugar simply dissolves in water (C). Vinegar (acetic acid) reacts with antacid tablets, producing salt, water, and non-toxic carbon dioxide gas (D). Nothing happens when table salt and rubbing alcohol are mixed (E)—there is no chemical reaction, and the salt does not dissolve.

61. A: According to the Köppen Climate Classification System, regions with continental climates are most commonly found in the interior regions of large landmasses. Continental climates are characterized by large seasonal temperature variations, with warm or hot summers and cold winters. Precipitation is often moderate and can occur throughout the year.

62. D: Blood is cooled as it passes through capillaries surrounding the sweat glands. Heat is absorbed along with excess salt and water and transferred to the glands as sweat. Droplets of sweat then evaporate from the skin surface to dissipate heat and cool the body. The kidney, bladder, and liver are not involved in regulating body temperature.

63. B: Proteins in the inner membrane of the mitochondrion accept high-energy electrons from NADH and $FADH_2$ and, in turn, transport protons from the matrix to the intermembrane space. The high proton concentration in the intermembrane space creates a gradient, which is harnessed by ATP synthase to produce ATP.

64. D: Conjugation is direct transfer of plasmid DNA between bacteria through a pilus. The F plasmid contains genes that enable bacteria to produce pili and is often the DNA that is transferred between bacteria.

65. A: Many organisms, especially organisms that live in harsh conditions such as deserts or frozen icy areas, have developed specific adaptations that allow them to survive. For example, cacti are able to expand to store large amounts of water, coyotes absorb some water from their food, and snakes can escape the heat by hiding within rocks.

66. C: Clouds form when water in the air condenses onto condensation nuclei in the air. Atmospheric water vapor will condense when the atmospheric temperature reaches the dew point.

67. C: Vectors are quantities with both magnitude and direction. Scalars are quantities with magnitude but not direction. Since velocity, acceleration, and force have magnitude and direction, they are all vectors. Since speed only has magnitude, speed is a scalar.

68. B: It is true that galaxies are gravitationally bound, so that structures within them orbit around the center. Galaxies do contain dark matter, and only the largest "giant" galaxies contain over one trillion stars. The smallest "dwarf" galaxies contain as few as 10 million stars. Clusters and superclusters are composed of many galaxies.

69. A: Since change in velocity divided by change in time equals acceleration, the slope of each line segment on this graph represents acceleration. Line segments I and IV both have zero slope, meaning there is no change in velocity over the time represented. No change in velocity means the velocity is constant; therefore, lines I and IV represent constant speed.

70. A: The majority of weather phenomena occur in the Earth's troposphere. The troposphere is the lowest layer of the atmosphere, extending from Earth's surface up to roughly 8–15 kilometers in altitude. It contains the majority of the mass of Earth's atmosphere and 99 percent of its water vapor.

71. C: A solute is a substance that is dissolved in another substance. In this case, the solute is the spices

72. A: Pioneer species colonize vacant habitats, and the first such species in a habitat demonstrate primary succession. Succession on rock or lava often begins with lichens. Lichens need very little organic material and can erode rock into soil to provide a growth substrate for other organisms.

73. B: Light travels in straight lines. As light moves from one substance to another, the light rays bend according to the refractive index of each substance. As the light travels through the air, it hits the non-submerged portion of the pencil. The light is reflected from the pencil and this is what we see. However, as the light travels *into* the water, the light waves are bent (refracted), and that light is subsequently reflected and travels to our eyes. What we perceive is a pencil that is no longer whole and straight, but broken and bent. It is refraction that causes this perception.

Although the other distractors are also properties of waves, they are not the reasons why the observer perceives the pencil as bent.

74. A: Coral reefs are destroyed by increased temperatures resulting from global warming and water pollution, which suffocates the coral as algae grows over it. Illegal collection and sale of coral to restaurants, pet stores, and others have depleted healthy colonies. Many conservation efforts have been started in recent years, including enacting international laws to protect the reefs, creating natural parks, and reattaching salvaged coral colonies on the reef with the hopes of reconstructing the reef.

75. C: Hund's rule states that electrons must populate empty orbitals of similar energy before pairing up. The Aufbau principle states that electrons must fill lower energy orbitals before filling higher energy orbitals. The Pauli Exclusion Principle states that no two electrons in the same atom can have the same four quantum numbers, and, therefore, two electrons in the same orbital will have opposite spins.

76. D: *Genetic engineering* is a general term to describe altering DNA sequences through adding or removing pieces of DNA from a native sequence. In the earliest genetic engineering processes, restriction enzymes were used to perform this "clipping" function, but other methods have been devised and are in use today. Current technologies include those using nucleases (such as CRISPR-Cas9, zinc-finger nucleases, or TALENs) or site-specific recombinases.

77. D: Although all of the answers are celestial bodies, natural bodies outside of the earth's atmosphere, one most strongly influences the earth's tides. The Sun's gravity also affects tides, but the Moon has a larger effect because it is much closer to Earth. The moon's gravitational pull on the earth causes the seas to rise and fall as one large wave, known as a tide, with a very large wavelength as compared to waves formed by wind.

78. D: The equation $6CO_2 + 6H_2O + \text{Energy} = C_6H_{12}O_6 + 6O_2$ (photosynthesis) can be balanced by counting the number of each element on the reactant side and comparing those totals to the product side. There should be equal numbers of each element on both sides, and they can be adjusted by changing the coefficient to add another molecule to the formula to balance the other side.

79. D: Reproductive habits would not be considered evidence for evolution. Usually, how a species reproduces does not support nor add to the body of evidence for the theory of evolution. Reproductive habits might exemplify how any given organism can adapt to changes in its environment as a way to survive. This does not necessarily show evolution. Fossil record is evidence for evolution as it shows evolutionary change of organisms over time. DNA sequences show that organisms that are related evolutionarily also have related gene sequences. Anatomical structures such as having an internal bony structure provide evidence of descent from a common ancestor.

80. A: Glaciers move because they are incredibly heavy, and the force of gravity slowly pulls them lower. Erosion is a result rather than a cause of glacier movement. Although large glaciers may only move a few inches a year or may not move at all, some valley glaciers in Europe move as much as 600 feet annually. The result is a rounded valley and a trail of rock and soil debris known as a moraine. The Great Lakes in the United States were formed by the passage of glaciers long ago.

81. C: All line segments on this graph represent acceleration since change in velocity divided by time equals acceleration. The line with the steepest slope represents the greatest acceleration. The steepest line is V, so option C is the correct answer.

82. A: Heat is absorbed by the solid during melting; therefore, ΔH is positive. Going from a solid to a liquid greatly increases the freedom of the particles, which increases the entropy, so ΔS is also positive.

83. A: A characteristic of a reputable scientific journal is that there is peer review of the quality of the research. The other choices may be characteristics of scientific journals, but these do not necessarily mean a journal is reputable.

84. D: Corundum and magnetite are oxides. Corundum is aluminum oxide, and magnetite is an iron oxide. Halides contain a halogen. Silicates contain silicon and oxygen (e.g., quartz and opal). Native elements such as copper and silver exist as uncombined elements.

85. D: Combustion of coal releases significant amounts of Hg into the atmosphere. When the Hg settles into the water, it becomes methylated and concentrates in fish, making them toxic to eat.

86. C: When a nucleus emits an alpha particle, its nucleon number decreases by four. An alpha particle is two protons bound together with two neutrons. Since it doesn't have any electrons, it has a charge of +2. Emitting an alpha particle causes the atomic number of the nucleus to decrease by two, and its mass to decrease by approximately four atomic mass units. Exactly how much the mass decreases depends on the binding energies of the two nuclei. Its charge decreases by two.

87. C: A salt is a neutral ionic compound consisting of a positively charged cation balanced with an equivalent amount of a negatively charged anion. Although it is very common for a salt to be composed of a metal and a nonmetal, this is not always true, as in the case of the salt ammonium acetate. The ammonium (NH_4^+) and acetate (CH_3COO^-) ions are both polyatomic ions composed of only nonmetals. Likewise, many salts are composed of an alkali or alkaline earth metal and a halogen, but this is not always the case.

88. A: The total energy of an isolated system is always conserved. However, the mechanical energy may not be, since some mechanical energy could be converted into radiation (light) or heat (through friction). According to Einstein's famous equation $E = mc^2$, where E is energy, m is mass, and c is the speed of light, energy can be converted into mass, and vice versa (like in nuclear reactions). This does not affect the conservation of energy law, however, since the mass is considered to have an energy equivalent. This equation does not tell anything about the mechanical energy of a particle; it just shows how much energy would be generated if the mass was converted directly into energy.

89. D: The frequency of ocean waves is measured by the number of wave crests that pass a given point each second. The crest of a wave is its highest point, and the trough is its lowest point. The horizontal distance between two subsequent crests is called wavelength, and the height is the vertical distance between a single wave's trough and crest.

90. C: A chemical change involves a chemical reaction where new products are formed. When silver tarnishes, a thin layer of corrosion is formed, indicating a chemical change. A physical change does not produce new substances. Phase changes such as evaporation and sublimation are examples of physical changes. Salt dissolving in water is also a physical change because the ions just separate, and no new substances are formed.

91. B: In numbers with decimals, the number of significant figures is determined by starting at the first nonzero digit on the left and counting to the last digit on the right. The number 0.003020 has 4 significant figures. The number 3,020.5 has 5 significant figures. The number 3.2005 has 5 significant figures. The number 0.0325 has 3 significant figures.

92. A: Pros of wind energy include space efficiency, no pollution, and low operational costs. Cons of wind energy include wind fluctuation, threats to wildlife, and the expense to manufacture and install.

93. A: The field of view is the diameter of the circle of light that is seen when one looks into the microscope. As the power of the objective increases, the field of view gets smaller. Therefore, the objective with the greatest field of view is the one with the lowest power.

94. A: Anthophyta is a division of plants that produces seeds as part of reproduction. Spermatopyta is the broader group that includes all plants that produce seeds for reproduction, which includes gymnosperms and angiosperms (the same group as anthophyta). Anthophyta are also known as the group that contains flowering plants. It is the largest and most diverse grouping of plants and includes many food, clothing, and medicinal uses for humans. Grains, beans, nuts, fruits, vegetables, spices, tea, coffee, chocolate, cotton, linen, and aspirin are all derived from plants from anthophyta. Lycophyta is a small group of plants including club mosses and scale trees. Sphenophyta contains about thirty species including horsetails, foxtails, or scouring rushes. Pterophyta contains non-seed plants like ferns. Lycophyta, sphenophyta, and pterophyta all use spores to reproduce sexually.

95. A: The relationship between wavelength and frequency is inversely proportional, and in general, the speed of sound is constant for almost all frequencies. So, the relationship between all three is defined to be: frequency times wavelength is equal to the speed of sound in a given medium, or $f \times \lambda = v$.

96. A: Orange red stars have temperatures less than 3,700 K. Yellow orange stars range between 3,700 and 5,200 K. Yellow white stars range between 5,200 and 6,000 K. Blue white stars range between 10,000 and 30,000 K.

97. C: The Mesozoic era is composed of the Triassic, Jurassic, and Cretaceous periods. It was preceded by the Paleozoic era, of which the Permian is the last period. The Triassic period ended about 200 million years ago, and was followed by the Jurassic period. The Jurassic period gave way to the Cretaceous period just under 150 million years ago.

98. B: When an astronomer observing stars detects a blue shift, he can conclude the star is moving closer or toward him. This is an example of the practical application of the Doppler effect in astronomy as applied to electromagnetic waves. The Doppler effect explains the change of wavelength caused by motion of the source or the relative difference in velocity between the observer and the source. When observing stars, a red shift or blue shift can be used to measure the speed that stars and galaxies are approaching or receding. Blue light has a higher frequency than red light. A red shift indicates a receding source.

99. B: The abiotic factors of an ecosystem are not alive; hence (A) is incorrect. Abiotic factors include such things as the atmosphere, water, soil, sunlight, temperatures, nutrient cycles, etc. While not living themselves, abiotic factors *do* affect the living organisms (C) in the ecosystem. Living organisms are biotic factors, including humans, other animals, plants, *and* microorganisms; hence abiotic factors do NOT include microorganisms (D).

100. D: Isotopes of the same element must have the same chemical behavior, and (A), (B), and (C) all represent, in one form or another, chemical behavior. Isotopes differ in mass, and this can be used to separate them by some appropriate physical property.

101. A: Long-term energy storage in animals takes the form of fat. Animals also store energy as glycogen, and plants store energy as starch, but these substances are for shorter-term use. Fats are a good storage form for chemical energy because fatty acids bond to glycerol in a condensation reaction to form fats (triglycerides). This reaction, which releases water, allows for the compacting of high-energy fatty acids in a concentrated form.

102. A: Appropriate laboratory safety rules should include instructions to always notify the instructor in case of any emergency. In the case of a fire, the instructor should be notified first. Then appropriate measures can be taken to actually put out the fire.

103. B: Unlike other organic molecules, lipids are not water soluble. They are largely nonpolar, and therefore hydrophobic. Lipids are not built from repeating monomers; this is characteristic of carbohydrates, proteins, and amino acids. Enzymes are proteins that can catalyze reactions. Lipids store more energy per gram than carbohydrates and proteins.

104. B: Electricity requires an energy source such as a generator to make it flow. It needs a conductor as a medium through which it can travel from place to place. An insulator (A and C)is a material that *blocks* the conduction of electricity. Insulation is used to prevent electricity from going where we do not want it to go—for example, into our bodies. Therefore, (D) is incorrect.

105. B: Plutonic, or intrusive, rock forms deep beneath the Earth's surface and cools slowly. Volcanic, or extrusive, rock solidifies at or near the surface. Hypabyssal rock forms below the Earth's surface but not at a depth as great as plutonic rock. Detrital rock is a type of sedimentary rock.

106. D: The average salinity of seawater is 3.5%. This can also be written as 35 parts per thousand or 3.5 parts per hundred.

107. B: Conduction is the transfer and distribution of heat energy from one molecule to the next within a substance. The spoon becomes warmer because the heat from the soup is conducted along the spoon. Convection is the transfer of heat energy in a gas or liquid through the movement of currents. Radiation is the transfer of heat through empty space in the form of rays or waves. Advection is the transfer of heat or other atmospheric properties by the horizontal movement of air.

108. B: When scientists and students are able to identify patterns and find meaning in the results of their experiments, they are using the process skill of Inference. When they use the results of their experiments to formulate new hypotheses (A), they are using the process skill of Prediction. When they identify the properties of objects or situations using their senses, they are using the process skill of Observation. When they report the results of their experiments and their conclusions based on these results to others (D), they are using the process skill of Communication. These skills are required for solving both math and science problems.

109. A: Fission is a nuclear process where atomic nuclei split apart to form smaller nuclei. Nuclear fission can release large amounts of energy, emit gamma rays, and form daughter products. It is used in nuclear power plants and bombs. Choice B, fusion, refers to a nuclear process whereby atomic nuclei join to form a heavier nucleus, such as with stars. This can release or absorb energy depending upon the original elements. Choice C, decay, refers to an atomic nucleus spontaneously losing energy and emitting ionizing particles and radiation. Choice D, ionization, refers to a process by which atoms obtain a positive or negative charge because the number of electrons does not equal that of protons.

110. C: The Earth's magnetic field protects it from solar wind. Solar wind is a stream of highly charged radioactive particles that emanate from the Sun, and these particles are deflected by the magnetic field. The magnetic field is shaped like a bowl that covers the side of the Earth facing the Sun. It deflects most solar particles, but some are trapped in the Van Allen belt. Particularly strong bursts of solar wind allow particles to pass through this belt into the Earth's ionosphere and upper atmosphere, creating geomagnetic storms and auroras.

111. D: The Cretaceous-Tertiary event, during which non-avian dinosaurs became extinct, occurred approximately 65.5 million years ago. It is the most recent of the five major extinction events that have occurred throughout the Earth's history.

112. D: The physical structure of the universe is thought to consist of filaments (walls of superclusters, clusters, and galaxies) that surround large, bubble-like voids. Filaments are the largest structures in the universe, with some forming huge structures like the Great Wall and the Sloan Great Wall.

113. D: According to Boyle's law, the volume of a gas is inversely proportional to pressure. As pressure increases, volume decreases. According to Avogadro's law, the volume of a gas is proportional to the number of moles. As the number of moles increases, volume increases. According to Charles's law, the volume of a gas is proportional to the temperature in kelvins. As the temperature increases, volume increases. Since temperature is a measure of the kinetic energy of a gas, volume is proportional to the kinetic energy.

114. C: Pollination is the transfer of pollen from the anther, the male part of the flower, to the stigma, the female part of the flower. This transfer can be accomplished either by wind, animals, or water. None of the other choices are involved in pollination: the xylem and petiole are structural and transport tissues; the apical and floral meristems are growth regions; root hairs absorb water, and stroma is part of the chloroplast.

115. A: Magnetic poles occur in pairs known as magnetic dipoles. Individual atoms can be considered magnetic dipoles due to the spin and rotation of the electrons in the atoms. When the dipoles are aligned, the material is magnetic. Choices B, C, and D are all magnetic materials. Therefore, the magnetic dipoles in these materials are not randomly aligned. Only choice A has randomly aligned dipoles.

116. A: The appearance of the Coriolis effect in the Earth's oceans is caused by the Earth's rotation. The Coriolis effect results when free objects such as water move over a rotating surface such as the Earth. As water moves from the poles towards the equator, it curves slightly westward, while water moving in the opposite direction (from the equator towards the poles) moves slightly eastward.

117. C: Translation is the process of the tRNA bringing the correct amino acid to the ribosome according to the sequence of the mRNA. Since translation only involves RNA, the four bases are adenine (A), cytosine (C), guanine (G), and uracil (U). There is no thymine (T) used in RNA. Cytosine (C) and guanine (G) pair and adenine (A) and uracil (U) pair. A codon is the triplet sequence that represents a specific amino acid or a start/stop point. It is on the messenger RNA (mRNA). The anticodon is on tRNA and corresponds to the amino acid used by the ribosome during translation. They are complementary. UGC becomes AUG; AUG becomes CGA. The mRNA codon sequence is U G C A U G C G A if the anticodon sequence formed during translation is A C G U A C G C U.

118. A: Water actually has its lowest volume at four degrees Celsius. Water stops contracting at four degrees Celsius. Water expands as it cools from four degrees Celsius to zero degrees Celsius.

119. D: Endocytosis is a process by which cells absorb larger molecules or even tiny organisms, such as bacteria, that would not be able to pass through the plasma membrane. Endocytic vesicles containing molecules from the extracellular environment often undergo further processing once they enter the cell.

120. A: Sublimation is the process of a solid changing directly into a gas without entering the liquid phase. Fusion refers to melting a solid into a liquid. Diffusion is the process of a material dispersing throughout another. Condensation is generally a gas turning into a liquid.

121. A: Isotopes are two atoms of the same element that have different mass. They have the same number of protons but a different number of neutrons. Choice C accurately describes ions. The other choices are incorrect.

122. B: The gastrula is the first three-layered stage of the embryo, containing the ectoderm, mesoderm, and endoderm.

123. D: Radiation therapy kills cells by damaging the DNA directly or by producing free radicals that damage the cells. Radiation therapy can kill normal cells. Radiation therapy can be used to cure cancer, prevent cancer from returning, shrink tumors, and reduce pain.

124. A: An inch is about $2.54 \text{ cm} = 25.4 \text{ mm} = 2.54 \times 10^{-5} \text{ km} = 2.54 \times 10^{-2} \text{ m}$.

125. D: Meiosis produces cells that are genetically different, having half the number of chromosomes of the parent cells. Mitosis produces cells that are genetically identical; daughter cells have the exact same number of chromosomes as parent cells. Mitosis is useful for repairing the body while meiosis is useful for sexual reproduction.

126. A: Chemical compounds are formed when valence electrons from atoms of two different elements are shared or transferred. Valence electrons are the electrons located in the outermost shell of the atom, and they occupy the highest energy level. Atoms may form compounds by sharing valence electrons (covalent bonding) or by transferring electrons.

127. D: A complete metamorphosis, as butterflies and mosquitoes undergo, includes the stages of egg (A), larva (B), pupa (D), and imago (C) or adult form. Insects such as grasshoppers, dragonflies, and cockroaches undergo an incomplete metamorphosis: they do not go through the stage of a pupa, which is typically inactive, does not feed, and stays hidden until the adult (imago) stage. The butterfly pupa is called a chrysalis. The mosquito pupa is called a tumbler.

128. D: Lower seed dispersal is not an advantage that angiosperms show over other types of plants. Gymnosperms, for example, have plentiful amounts of pollen, but it does not always hit its mark. Angiosperms are the most recently evolved plant division and contain at least 260,000 extant species. They are very diverse and occupy many habitats. Many other species in other plant divisions do not have true leaves. Gymnosperms have modified leaves in the form of needles. Double fertilization refers to how one sperm cell fuses with an ovule, forming the zygote. The second sperm forms into a triploid endosperm that provides energy for the embryo.

129. C: Sources of renewable energy include geothermal power, solar energy, and wind power. Sources of nonrenewable energy include nuclear power and fossil fuels like coal, natural gas, and crude oil.

130. B: A barometer is an instrument for measuring atmospheric pressure, used especially in weather forecasting.

131. D: Operons are common in prokaryotes. They are units of DNA that control the transcription of DNA and code for their own regulatory proteins as well as structural proteins.

132. C: Graham's law of diffusion allows one to calculate the relative diffusion rate between two different gases based on their masses.

133. B: Newton's First law of motion states *both* that an object at rest tends to stay at rest (A), and an object in motion tends to stay in motion (C), unless or until an opposing force changes this. Newton's *Third law of motion* states that for every action there is an equal and opposite reaction (D).

134. B: According to the first law of planetary motion, planets move in elliptical orbits, not circular. According to the second law of planetary motion, a radius vector connecting a planet to the sun sweeps out equal areas in equal amounts of time. According to the third law of planetary motion, the square of the period of a planet is directly proportional to the cube of the mean distance.

135. D: The phloem is the pipeline through which carbohydrates are transported to the roots. It is located outside of the xylem and lives for only a short time before becoming part of the outer bark.

136. C: Tropical climate zones are characterized by frequent rainfall, especially during the monsoon season, and by moderate temperatures that vary little from season to season or between night and day. Tropical zones do experience frequent rainfall, which leads to abundant vegetation.

137. D: The colors of the visible spectrum from the lowest to highest frequency are red, orange, yellow, green, blue, and violet. Therefore, violet has the highest frequency.

138. A: Radioactive decay converts mass into energy ($E = mc^2$). The mass of products is always less than that of the starting materials since some mass is now energy.

139. C: In respiration, food is used to produce energy as glucose and oxygen that react to produce carbon dioxide, water and ATP

140. A: A double concave lens is a diverging lens in which the light rays are spread apart. Therefore, the image formed by a double concave lens is always reduced, upright, and virtual regardless of the distance of the object from the lens.

141. C: Eyewash stations should be capable of delivered rinsing fluid to both eyes for a minimum of 15 minutes. The stations should be located in an accessible area where a person can reach the station in no more than 10 seconds.

142. B: When the accumulation of snow and ice exceeds ablation, a glacier will gradually form. Ablation is the sloughing off of ice and snow through melting, evaporation, sublimation, and wind erosion. When snow and ice accumulate faster than ablation occurs, a glacier will form and continue to gain mass until the rate of ablation overtakes the rate of accumulation.

143. D: Since there are twice as many molecules of hydrogen as molecules of oxygen, the partial pressure of hydrogen will be greater. The mass of hydrogen will not be greater than the mass of oxygen present even though there are more moles of hydrogen, due to oxygen having a higher molecular weight. Each gas will occupy the same volume. Hydrogen and oxygen gas can coexist in the container without reacting to produce water. There is no indication given that a chemical reaction has occurred.

144. D: Photosynthesis is the process by which plants generate their own food (glucose), using sunlight, water, and carbon dioxide. Oxygen is also generated as a byproduct.

145. A: Since the atomic number is 20, which represents the number of protons in the atom, there must be an equal number of electrons in a neutral atom. Protons have a positive charge and electrons are negative. Equal numbers of protons and electrons will result in a neutral atom, or zero charge.

146. B: According to the law of universal gravitation, the force of attraction between two objects is inversely proportional to the square of the distance between the two objects. If the distance increases, the force decreases. If the distance is doubled, the force is reduced to one-fourth of the original amount.

147. D: Within a habitat, there is a maximum number of individuals that can continue to thrive, known as the habitat's carrying capacity. When the population size approaches this number, population growth will stop.

148. B: Darwin studied Lyell's work *Principles of Geology* while sailing around South America and the Galapagos Islands. Lyell's theory of uniformitarianism supposes that all things are continuing in the same uniform natural processes and that the changes to the Earth's crust have arisen from these continuous, uniform processes. Darwin was inspired by this theory and used it as a foundation for his theory of evolution, adopting the phrase that "the present is the key to the past" to the evolutionary history of life on Earth. Choice C is incorrect because it reverses the phrase. Choice A is incorrect because uniformitarianism is completely opposed to the idea of catastrophism, which argues that the majority of Earth's features are a result of violent, sudden events, such as meteorites and other natural disasters. Finally, D is incorrect because natural selection states that the fittest organisms will survive to reproduce.

149. D: A chemical reaction will always have an endothermic (absorb energy) or exothermic (release energy) reaction, and a chemical equation must always be balanced; therefore, the reactants and products will always be equal, resulting in a modification of the arrangement of the atoms and a change in energy.

150. B: Photosynthesis converts carbon dioxide into sugars that plants use. Three types of photosynthesis are C3, C4, and CAM. C3 is used by most plants. C4 plants live in areas with high temperatures and high light exposure. C4 first forms a four-carbon sugar instead of the three-carbon sugar formed by C3. Also, the stomata of C4 plants are faster at absorbing carbon dioxide and do not have to open as long, so less water is lost by transpiration. A C4 plant, such as saltbush, corn, or some grasses, would live in a very hot environment rather than a cold, marine, or dark environment. Plants that use the CAM (Crassulacean Acid Metabolism) type of photosynthesis also use water more efficiently as their stomata are closed during the day and open at night. Desert cacti are examples.

151. C: In humans, diploid cells are those that contain 46 chromosomes. There are 23 pairs of chromosomes each made up of one chromosome from the father and one from the mother. In meiosis I, each chromosome replicates itself and lines up, or synapses, with its homologous chromosome, and each of the daughter cells ends up with one copy of each of the chromosomes. The two daughter cells at the end of meiosis I are haploid because they contain half of the chromosomes of the parent cell. In humans, this would be 23 chromosomes. However, each of these chromosomes are made of two sister chromatids. In meiosis II, the sister chromatids in the daughter cells separate and result in the production of the gametes. These are also haploid cells because they contain one copy of half of the genetic material of the parent cell. Four haploid cells result from meiosis. Choice A, mitosis, can be eliminated as it refers to the process of cell division where each daughter cell contains exactly the same genetic material as the parent cell. Choice B, telophase, refers to phases of both mitosis and meiosis, during which chromosomes move toward the opposite ends of the cell.

152. D: A covalent bond is one in which atoms share valence electrons. Within a water molecule, one oxygen atom and two hydrogen atoms share valence electrons to yield the H_2O structure.

153. B: The temperature systems of Kelvin and Celsius use the same unit size, but they have different zeroes. In order to convert from Kelvin to Celsius, simply subtract 273. In this case, $119 - 273 = -154$, so 119 K is equivalent to -154 degrees Celsius.

154. B: Metamorphic rock is produced when a protolith undergoes profound changes after being exposed to extreme heat and pressure. A protolith is any rock that is transformed through this process. The original rock may be sedimentary, igneous, or metamorphic. The extreme heat and pressure that serve as the catalyst for this transformation may be produced by the intrusion of magma or tectonic activity, among other factors.

155. D: Once a hypothesis has been verified and accepted, it becomes a theory. A theory is a generally accepted explanation that has been highly developed and tested. A theory can explain data and be expected to predict outcomes of tests. A fact is considered to be an objective and verifiable observation, whereas a scientific theory is a greater body of accepted knowledge, principles, or relationships that might explain a fact. A law is an explanation of events for which the outcome is always the same. A conclusion is more of an opinion and could be based on observation, evidence, fact, laws, or even beliefs.

156. D: When diluting acids, the acid should always be added to the water. This way, if splashing occurs, only water is splashed out of the beaker. Additionally, this procedure ensures that only a small amount of acid is present in a much larger volume of water. This is especially important when diluting sulfuric acid, because large amounts of heat may be released in the hydration process, which could cause a small amount of water to boil rapidly.

157. A: The period of a simple pendulum depends on the length and the rate of acceleration due to gravity. The period is independent of amplitude (to a good approximation) for amplitudes less than about 15 degrees. The period of a pendulum is unaffected by increasing the mass.

158. D: The equation for power, $power = \frac{work}{time}$, can be utilized. The mass of the object (10 kg) and the distance (10 m) can be used to calculate work, $work = mass \times (gravitational\ acceleration) \times distance$. The value for time is provided.

159. B: According to the Dana classification system, gold, silver, and copper belong to the elemental class. Members of the oxide class include chromite and magnetite, and hydrocarbons and acetates are members of the organic class. Sulfide minerals include pyrite and galena.

160. B: In a nuclear chain reaction, free neutrons released from nuclear fission cause a nucleus to split and release more neutrons.

Practice Test #2

1. When fault-block mountains like those in the Western United States are formed, sections that are lifted by tensional forces are called:

a. Antiforms
b. Faces
c. Horsts
d. Rifts

Refer to the following for questions 2–3:

A biome featuring scrubby plants and small evergreen trees has a hot, dry summer followed by a wetter winter. The following food chain exists in the biome:

$$tree \rightarrow caterpillar \rightarrow frog \rightarrow snake \rightarrow hawk \rightarrow vulture \rightarrow worm$$

2. Which biome is this?

a. Taiga
b. Coniferous forest
c. Chaparral
d. Savanna

3. What role do vultures play in the food chain?

a. Scavengers
b. Detritivores
c. Primary carnivores
d. Herbivores

4. What is a potential drawback that medical advances could have for human life?

a. Medical advances require humans to constantly re-examine their moral beliefs.
b. Medical advances have drastically increased the human life span, placing stress on the environment and the economy.
c. While medical advances have cured many diseases, new diseases may still arise and threaten lives.
d. Medical advances have given people many more opportunities for treatments and drugs depending on what they can afford.

5. What other planet in the solar system experiences a greenhouse effect similar to that observed on Earth?

a. Mercury
b. Venus
c. Neptune
d. Saturn

6. A worker applies a force of 500.0 N to a pulley for a distance of 1.5 m to move a crate that weighs 1,000.0 N a distance of 0.5 m. What is the ideal mechanical advantage of this pulley?

a. 4
b. 2
c. 3
d. 5

7. Which of the following is an example of a density-dependent limiting factor?

a. Air pollution by a factory
b. The toxic effect of waste products
c. Nearby volcanic eruptions
d. Frosts

8. Which statement best explains the Biological Species Concept (BSC)?

a. It states that the status of species is based on the ability to pass on the most successful traits to their offspring.
b. It states that the status of species is based on the reproductive isolation of populations.
c. It states that the status of species is based on the ability of populations to mix and produce fertile hybrids.
d. It states that the status of a species is due to the theory of natural selection.

9. Which of the following organisms is likely to have the greatest quantity of mercury in its body?

a. Mosquitoes
b. Frogs
c. Filter-feeding fish
d. Fish-eating birds

10. Which of the following descriptions concerning air masses is true?

a. Maritime tropical air masses bring warm, dry weather.
b. Continental polar air masses bring warm, moist weather.
c. Continental tropical air masses bring cold, dry weather.
d. Maritime polar air masses bring cold, moist weather.

11. Which type of plant does NOT produce seeds?

a. Monocots
b. Angiosperms
c. Gymnosperms
d. Nonvascular plants

12. Which of the following statements about heat transfer is NOT true?

a. As the energy of a system changes, its thermal energy must change or work must be done.
b. Heat transfer from a warmer object to a cooler object can occur spontaneously.
c. Heat transfer can never occur from a cooler object to a warmer object.
d. If two objects reach the same temperature, energy is no longer available for work.

13. For the gas phase reaction $CH_4 + 4Cl_2 \rightarrow CCl_4 + 4HCl$, what would be the equilibrium expression K_{eq} for this reaction?

a. $\frac{[CH_4][Cl_2]}{[CCl_4][4HCl]}$
b. $\frac{[CH_4][Cl_2]}{[CCl_4][HCl]^4}$
c. $\frac{[4Cl][CCl_4]}{[CH_4][4HCl]}$
d. $\frac{[CCl_4][HCl]^4}{[CH_4][Cl_2]^4}$

14. What laboratory practice can increase the precision of a measurement?

a. Repeating the measurement several times
b. Calibrating the equipment each time you use it
c. Using metric measuring devices
d. Reading the laboratory instructions before the lab

15. How is light created in the core of the Sun?

a. Convection
b. Fission reactions
c. Fusion reactions
d. Chemical reactions

16. Fossils are least likely to be found in which type of rock?

a. Sedimentary rock
b. Metamorphic rock
c. Igneous rock
d. Fossils are commonly found in all types of rock

17. Consider the following statements about Newton's law:

I. A newton is a fundamental unit.
II. Mass and acceleration are inversely related when the force is constant.
III. Newton's first law can be derived from Newton's second law.
IV. Newton's second law can be derived from the universal law of gravity.

Which of the statements are true?

a. I, II, and III.
b. II and III only.
c. III only.
d. None of them

18. According to the geologic time scale, which of the following statements is NOT true?

a. The rise of human civilization occurred between 6,000 and 12,000 years ago.
b. The Cambrian explosion occurred after the Jurassic Period.
c. Amphibians appeared before reptiles, mammals, and birds.
d. The origin of the first cells occurred approximately 4,000,000,000 years ago.

19. Which of the following is NOT supported by Dalton's atomic theory of matter?

a. Differences in properties of elements are due to differences in the atoms of the elements.
b. Atoms of a particular element all have the same properties, such as size and mass.
c. Every element consists of tiny particles called atoms, which can be split into even smaller pieces.
d. Chemical processes result from the rearrangement, combination, and separation of atoms.

20. Which of the following is the most likely explanation for the reason finches on separate islands within an archipelago have differently shaped beaks?

a. Each bird evolved from a pre-existing ancestor on each island
b. The finches spread among the islands, but in small numbers, so genetic drift caused beak shape to change
c. Natural selection shaped the beaks in accordance with food availability on each island
d. The different finches were introduced by ancient humans

21. Two species of finches are able to utilize the same food supply, but their beaks are different. They are able to coexist on an island because of:

a. Niche overlap
b. Character displacement
c. Resource partitioning
d. Realized niches

22. For the reaction $CO_2(g) + H_2(g) \rightleftharpoons CO(g) + H_2O(l)$, which of the following will occur if the pressure of the reaction is increased?

a. The reaction order will increase.
b. The forward reaction rate will decrease.
c. The reaction equilibrium will shift to the right.
d. The reaction will stop.

23. Which of the following ethical questions regarding biotechnology would be answered and regulated by the Food and Drug Administration?

a. Should the packaging of meat products that come from cloned animals be labeled?
b. Should nitrate or sulfate fertilizers be added to oil spills to assist the decomposition of crude oil by bacteria?
c. Should parents be allowed to genetically alter an embryo by choosing its physical characteristics?
d. Should cells or components of cells be used to create industrially useful products?

24. How do the hydrogen bonds in water affect its characteristics?

a. Hydrogen bonds are so polar that they can attract non-polar molecules.
b. Hydrogen bonds cause water to be denser when it is a solid than when it is a liquid.
c. Hydrogen bonds cause water to have a high enough surface tension that some organisms can move across it.
d. Hydrogen bonds cause water to be a poor solvent.
e. Hydrogen bonds make water an excellent buffer.

25. Which of the following is an example of the alternation of generations life cycle?

a. Asexual reproduction of strawberries by runners
b. Annual plants that live through a single growing season
c. Ferns that have a large diploid and a diminutive haploid stage
d. Insects that have distinct larval and adult stages

26. Which of the following is a proposed explanation for the formation of black holes?

a. High-energy collisions
b. Gravitational collapse
c. Accretion of matter
d. A and B

27. Which of the following elements do plants NOT need in order to undergo photosynthesis?

a. Carbon
b. Oxygen
c. Nitrogen
d. Hydrogen

28. Which of the following demographic changes would lead to a population with an older age composition?

a. Increased birth rate
b. Environmental pollution
c. Increased availability of food
d. Medical advancements that increase life expectancy

29. Which of the following parts of an angiosperm gives rise to the fruit?

a. Pedicel
b. Filament
c. Sepal
d. Ovary

Refer to the following for question 30:

Diagram representing a cross section of a tree trunk:

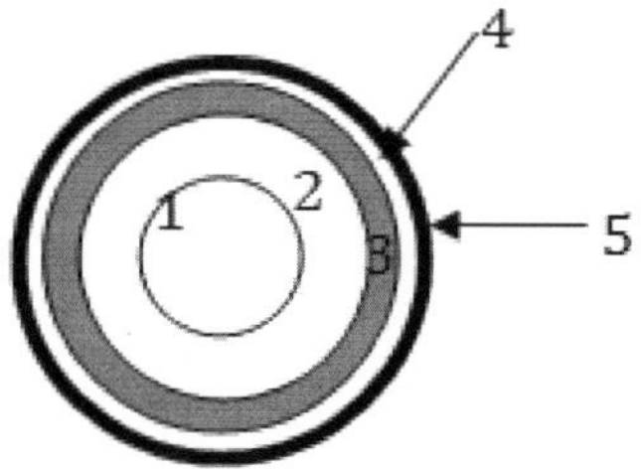

30. Which structure contains tissue that is dead at maturity?

a. 1
b. 2
c. 3
d. 4

31. Which of the following is NOT one of the five major physical properties of minerals?

a. Chemical composition
b. Hardness
c. Luster
d. Streak

32. Which of the following is considered observational evidence in support of the Big Bang Theory?

a. Expansion in the redshifts of galaxies
b. Measurements of cosmic microwave background radiation
c. Measurements of the distribution of quasars and galaxies
d. All of the above

33. Which of the following subatomic particles has the smallest mass?

a. Protons
b. Electrons
c. Quarks
d. Neutrons

34. Which structures on a leaf surface open to release water vapor during transpiration and close during drought?

a. Pith
b. Stomata
c. Guard cells
d. Sepals

35. What is the scientific definition of work?

a. The amount of energy used to accomplish a job
b. The force used to move a mass over a distance
c. The amount of energy used per unit of time
d. Energy stored in an object due to its position

36. What drives weather systems to move west to east in the mid-latitudes?

a. The prevailing westerlies
b. The prevailing easterlies
c. The trade winds
d. The doldrums

37. James Hutton is best known for:

a. Establishing the first observable evidence for the Big Bang Theory
b. Suggesting the Third Law of Thermodynamics
c. Proposing the theory of uniformitarianism
d. Introducing the Law of Superposition

38. Plants begin to break down the products of photosynthesis through respiration. What is the result of respiration?

a. Water
b. Oxygen and glucose
c. Carbon dioxide and sugar
d. Carbon dioxide and water

Refer to the following for question 39:

Guidelines for Field Journals

1. Always record the date, place, and time spent observing.
2. Describe the weather, including temperature, cloud cover, condensation, and winds, as well as any foreign (not natural) influences on the environment.

39. After their field trip, the students decide to work on a project together. Which of the following would be the best project, if its purpose were to protect biodiversity in its community?

a. Working together to improve the quality of food at the zoo.
b. Beginning a campaign to ban gas-motored boats from the pond.
c. Exploring water-treatment methods that are non-toxic.
d. Starting a recycling drive at school.

40. What type of change occurs when a liquid transitions to a gas?

a. A phase change
b. A chemical change
c. Sublimation
d. Condensation

41. The condition of balance and dynamic stability that characterizes living systems under normal conditions is called:

a. Homeostasis
b. Metabolism
c. Respiration
d. Symbiosis

42. An electron is moving in a straight line. Another particle is moving in a straight line parallel to the path of the electron but in the opposite direction. Initially the electron and particle are far apart, but get closer together. When the two particles are in the vicinity of one another, they experience an attractive magnetic force. Which of the following is a correct inference from this fact?

a. The particle has a north pole and a south pole.
b. The particle is positively charged.
c. The particle is negatively charged.
d. The particle has either a north pole or a south pole.

43. Which of the following is the greatest ethical controversy related to in vitro fertilization?

a. The fertilization outside of the mother's body
b. The multiple eggs produced by the ovary
c. The expense involved
d. The disposal of unused zygotes or embryos

44. Which of the following is true of a volcano that is thought to be dormant?

a. It will probably never erupt again, and it is quite safe for people to live near its base.
b. It is expected to erupt some time again in the future, but danger is not imminent.
c. It is expected to erupt soon, and evacuation should be commenced.
d. It is a shield volcano that is erupting, but people living near the volcano should not expect their lives to be significantly disrupted.

45. Which of the following subskills best fits the process skill of observing?

a. Using the five senses to collect evidence and write descriptions
b. Grouping objects based on similarities, differences, and interrelationships
c. Explaining or interpreting collected evidence
d. Reporting to others what has been found by experimentation

46. In resonance, small vibrations can produce a larger standing wave that becomes stronger than the original vibrations, assuming the vibrations are at the right frequency to generate resonance. If a pendulum is vibrated at a resonance frequency, what would you expect to happen?

a. The period of the pendulum will increase.
b. The time between swings will decrease.
c. The pendulum will swing higher.
d. The length of the pendulum will decrease.

47. Which statement is correct regarding the phenomenon of magnetism?

a. Opposite poles of magnets repel each other.
b. The like poles of magnets attract each other.
c. Magnets can attract/repel without touching.
d. Magnets work beyond their magnetic fields.

48. Which of the following body systems allows a person to move?

a. integumentary system
b. digestive system
c. endocrine system
d. muscular system

49. A liquid is heated from 50 °C to 80 °C. Which of the following statements is generally true about the solubility of solids and gases in the liquid?

a. The solubility of solids will increase, and the solubility of gases will decrease.
b. The solubility of solids will decrease, and the solubility of gases will increase.
c. The solubility of solids will increase, and the solubility of gases will increase.
d. The solubility of solids will decrease, and the solubility of gases will decrease.

50. Cardiac output is the product of what two factors?

a. Heart rate and stroke volume
b. Stroke volume and blood pressure
c. Heart rate and pulse
d. Stroke volume and oxygen consumption

51. How does the freezing point of sea water compare to that of fresh water?

a. Sea water has a higher freezing point.
b. Sea water has a lower freezing point.
c. They are the same.
d. Sea water does not freeze.

52. Describe the correct outer shell electronic arrangement of phosphorous.

a. $4s^2 4p^3$
b. $3s^2 3p^3$
c. $2s^2 3p^3$
d. $2s^2 2p^3$

53. Which of the following of Lamarck's evolutionary ideas turned out to be true?

a. Natural selection
b. Organisms naturally transform into increasingly complex organisms
c. Inheritance of acquired characters
d. Body parts develop with increased usage and weaken with disuse

54. Which of the following is true?

a. Materials whose atoms have strongly bound electrons conduct.
b. Materials whose atoms have loose electrons insulate electricity.
c. Materials with free electrons block the conduction of electricity.
d. Materials whose atoms feature tightly bound electrons insulate.

55. All of the following are examples of physical changes in the digestive system except:

a. Squeezing the food through the esophagus
b. Drinking to help aid in swallowing food
c. Chewing food into smaller pieces
d. Digestion of fat in the small intestine

56. The behaviors of living organisms are changed and shaped by:

a. Primarily internal stimuli
b. Primarily external stimuli
c. Preset genetic programs
d. Internal and external cues

57. Which of the following is a true statement about the Earth's oceans?

a. Oceans comprise about 50% of the Earth's surface.
b. The deepest point in the ocean is about 6,000 meters below sea level.
c. The ocean is divided geographically into four areas: the Atlantic, Pacific, Mediterranean, and Indian.
d. The ocean's salinity is usually between 34 and 35 parts per thousand, or 35,000 parts per million.

58. According to Ohm's Law, how are voltage and current related in an electrical circuit?

a. Voltage and current are inversely proportional to one another.
b. Voltage and current are directly proportional to one another.
c. Voltage acts to oppose the current along an electrical circuit.
d. Voltage acts to decrease the current along an electrical circuit.

59. What effect does science have on technology?

a. Science verifies what technology discovers
b. Technology often results from scientific discoveries
c. Science has no effect on technology; each is independent of the other
d. Scientific progress is dependent on technology

60. Which of the following is formed by meiosis?

a. spores
b. embryos
c. DNA
d. chromosomes

61. In the field of geology, the term "uniformitarianism" refers to the belief that:

a. Catastrophic events like mass extinctions are the main forces that have shaped the Earth.
b. The Earth's crust has not undergone any dramatic changes since its formation.
c. The natural forces that shape the Earth have remained relatively constant over geologic time.
d. The Earth's stratigraphy is more or less uniform at any given geographic location.

62. Which temperature scales have exactly 100 degrees between the freezing point and the boiling point of water?

a. Celsius only
b. Celsius and Kelvin
c. Celsius and Fahrenheit
d. Celsius, Fahrenheit, and Kelvin

Refer to the following for question 63:

A chemistry experiment is performed to determine the effect of a nonvolatile solute on the boiling point of water. Three trials are performed in which 10 mg, 20 mg, and 30 mg of salt are added to 500 mL of distilled water. Each solution is heated on a hot plate, and the elevated boiling points are recorded.

63. What is the purpose of conducting this experiment?

a. To test a hypothesis
b. To collect data
c. To identify a control state
d. To choose variables

64. In the marine waters, there is a beautiful, orange clown fish that lives closely with a sea anemone. This sea anemone can sting its prey with poisonous venom before devouring it; however, the clown fish is not affected by the sea anemone at all. The clown fish is only safe when hiding within the sea anemone's poisonous tentacles and protects the hiding spot from a certain type of fish who tries to eat the sea anemone. This is an example of what type of relationship?

a. Commensalism
b. Mutualism
c. Parasitism
d. None of the above

65. What type of compound is formed by the combination of two or more nonmetallic elements with one another?

a. Organic
b. Ionic
c. Covalent
d. Chemical

66. Any given temperature can be represented using three different temperature scales. Which temperature scale below yields a sequence of numbers from *lowest to highest* for the temperature of boiling water?

a. °C, °F, K
b. °F, °C, K
c. °F, K, °C
d. K, °C, °F
e. K, °F, °C

67. Students experimentally determine that the specific heat of copper is $0.410\ \frac{J}{g \cdot °C}$. If the known value of the specific heat of copper is $0.385\ \frac{J}{g \cdot °C}$, what is the percent error?

a. 6.10%
b. 16.4%
c. 6.49%
d. 15.4%

68. Which of the following is true of different isotopes of the same element?

a. It has a different number of protons than its element.
b. It has a different number of electrons than its element.
c. It has a different charge as compared to its element.
d. It has a different number of neutrons than other isotopes of the same element.

69. Which of the following conditions and chemical pairs is an example of a buffer?

a. Homeostasis; H_2CO_3/HCO_3^-
b. Water has a neutral pH; $(H_3O)^+/OH^-$
c. Copper can be electroplated onto tin; Cu^+/Sn^{2+}
d. Aluminum hydroxide is not soluble; Al^{3+}/OH^-

70. In the food chain pyramid above, which segment represents the placement of a coyote?

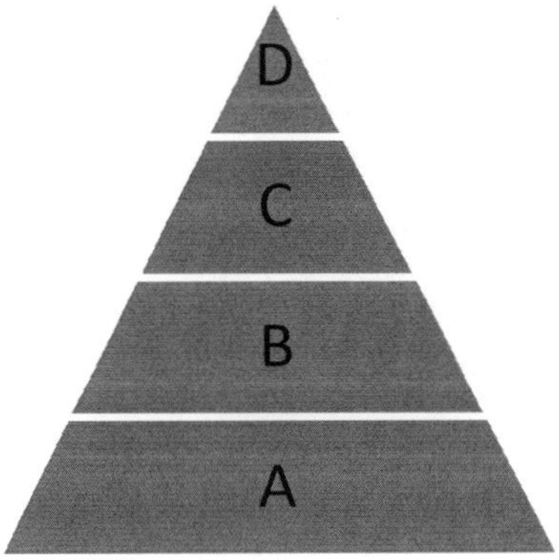

a. A (Producer)
b. B (Primary Consumer)
c. C (Secondary Consumer)
d. D (Decomposer)

71. Which of the following processes is an example of positive feedback?

a. High CO_2 blood levels stimulate respiration which decreases blood CO_2 levels
b. High blood glucose levels stimulate insulin release, which makes muscle and liver cells take in glucose
c. Increased nursing stimulates increased milk production in mammary glands
d. Low blood oxygen levels stimulate erythropoietin production which increases red blood cell production by bone marrow

72. Which of the following events directly results in a volcanic eruption?

a. A batholith forms beneath the Earth's surface.
b. Magma fills vertical and horizontal fractures in the Earth's crust, creating sills and dikes.
c. An oceanic plate is subducted by a continental plate.
d. A dike reaches the Earth's surface, and a plume passes through it.

73. In Lake Erie, a species of fish called the Blue Pike was overfished one year. The following year, there was a pollution incident that killed off another large portion of the population. These events, combined with the previous year's overfishing of adult fish, led to the extinction of the Blue Pike species—none of the other species were affected. What happened to other fish species in the lake over time after the Blue Pike became extinct?

a. They became extinct
b. They were not affected by the other species' fate
c. Their numbers increased due to lack of competition
d. Their numbers decreased due to lack of competition

74. Which of the following statements correctly describes an effect of the Gulf Stream?

a. It increases humidity along North America's west coast.
b. It makes the climate of South America colder.
c. It makes the climate of Northern Europe warmer.
d. It makes the climate of the Caribbean milder and less humid.

75. Which of the following creates an electromagnet?

a. Rapidly spinning and rotating electrons inside an iron bar
b. An iron bar moving inside a coil of wire that contains a current
c. The movement of electrons through a complete circuit
d. Convection currents within the liquid core of Earth's interior

76. Water is likely to have the shortest residence time in which of the following types of reservoirs?

a. A glacier
b. A lake
c. A river
d. The atmosphere

77. What is the result of allopatric speciation?

a. New species due to geographic isolation.
b. New species due to geographic overlap.
c. Hybrid species due to geographic overlap.
d. Loss of diversity of a species due to geographic divergence.

78. Which of the following substances has a pH closest to 1?

a. Bleach
b. Water
c. Ammonia
d. Vinegar

79. The synaptonemal complex is present in which of the following phases of the cell cycle?

a. Metaphase of mitosis
b. Prophase of meiosis I
c. Telophase of meiosis I
d. Metaphase of meiosis II

80. Which of the following is the correct definition of a conductor?

a. A metal wire in an electrical circuit.
b. A material that contains movable electric charges.
c. A material that is not a semiconductor or insulator.
d. Any device that allows electricity to flow.

81. Which of the following types of chemicals are considered generally unsafe to store together?

I. Liquids and solids
II. Acids and bases
III. Reducing agents and oxidizing agents
IV. Metals and salts

a. I, II
b. II, III
c. III, IV
d. I, IV

82. Physical weathering of rocks can be caused by all of the following EXCEPT:

a. The freezing and thawing of water on the surface of rocks
b. Changes in temperature
c. Oxidation
d. Changes in pressure due to the removal of overlying rocks

83. Which of Newton's laws explains why seatbelts are needed?

a. Second law of motion
b. Law of universal gravitation
c. First law of motion
d. Third law of motion

84. Which of the following has the potential for negative impacts including soil contamination, surface water contamination, pollution, and leachate?

a. Landfills
b. Incinerators
c. Recycling centers
d. Irrigation systems

85. Which of the following radioactive emissions results in an increase in atomic number?

a. Alpha
b. Negative Beta
c. Positive Beta
d. Gamma

86. The masses of four different objects, taken with different scales, were 23.04 g, 7.12 g, 0.0088 g, and 5.423 g. What is the total mass of all four objects to the proper number of decimal places?

a. 35.59180 g
b. 35.5918 g
c. 35.60 g
d. 35.59 g

87. Which of the following is a serious direct impact of climate change?

a. Soil erosion
b. Deforestation
c. Water pollution
d. Increase in average sea level

88. Which part of a flower collects pollen?

a. Style
b. Stigma
c. Petals
d. Sepals

89. Magnesium metal is reacted with hydrobromic acid according to the following equation:

$$Mg + 2HBr \rightarrow MgBr_2 + H_2$$

If 100 g of Mg is reacted with 100 g of HBr, which statement about the reaction is true?

a. Mg is the limiting reagent.
b. HBr is the excess reagent.
c. Mg is the excess reagent.
d. 100 g of $MgBr_2$ will be produced.

90. A nucleus absorbs a neutron and undergoes a fission reaction. Which of the following statements explains why this happens?

a. The nucleus is more stable with the additional neutron.
b. The new nucleus is unstable.
c. Energy is released.
d. The binding energy per nucleon decreases.

91. A tapeworm lives within another organism and feeds off the nutrients that are ingested by that organism. At times, this can cause the organism to experience malnutrition or death. This is an example of what type of relationship?

a. Predator/prey
b. Symbiosis
c. Parasite/host
d. Producer/consumer

92. Which of the following is the best prediction for solubility at 150 degrees Celsius?

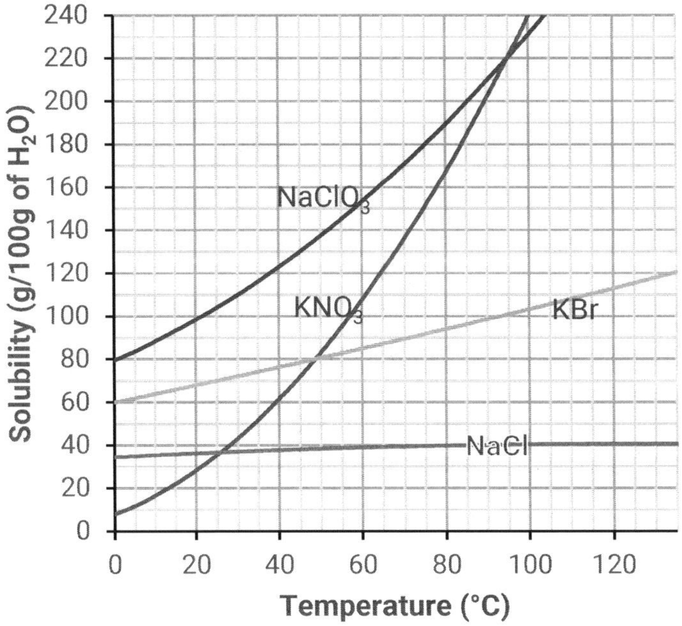

a. 260 g $NaClO_3$ per 100 g H_2O
b. 250 g KNO_3 per 100 g H_2O
c. 130 g KBr per 100 g H_2O
d. 80 g NaCl per 100 g H_2O

93. What are pure substances that consist of more than one type of atom?

a. Elements
b. Compounds
c. Molecules
d. Mixtures

94. A total solar eclipse can be observed only by viewers located:

a. Within the penumbra but outside of the umbra
b. Within the umbra
c. Within either the umbra or the penumbra
d. Outside of the Moon's penumbra

95. In mosses, eggs and sperm are produced by:

a. Spores
b. Sporophytes
c. Gametophytes
d. Zygotes

96. When a cold front begins to overtake a warm front, this results in what type of front?

a. Stationary front
b. Occluded front
c. Cold front
d. Warm front

97. Which of the following lessons would be the best set of examples illustrating the difference between scientific fact and theory?

a. Big Bang and Laws of Motion
b. Chaos theory and Evolution
c. Conservation of Mass/Electricity and Carbon-14 Dating
d. Astronomical Wormholes and Black Holes

98. If you were testing the effectiveness of a cream that reduced the signs of wrinkles around women's eyes, which of the following would be a good control group?

a. Rats with no wrinkles
b. A group of women with no wrinkles around their eyes who are given the cream
c. A group of women with wrinkles who are given a cream that has no effect
d. A group of women with wrinkles who are given a similar cream that's already on the market

99. The volume of water in a bucket is 2.5 liters. When an object with an irregular shape and a mass of 40 grams is fully submerged in the water, the total volume becomes 4.5 liters. What is the density of the object?

a. 0.1 g/L
b. 2 g/L
c. 20 g/L
d. 80 g/L

100. The density of a material refers to:

a. Mass per volume
b. Mass per mole
c. Molecular weight per volume
d. Moles per volume

101. The process whereby a radioactive element releases energy slowly over a long period of time to lower its energy and become more stable is best described as which of the following?

a. Combustion
b. Fission
c. Fusion
d. Decay

102. This organelle contains digestive enzymes that break down food and unneeded substances. They are also thought to be linked to the aging process. What part of a cell does this describe?

a. Lysosomes
b. Chromatin
c. Plastids
d. Golgi apparatus

103. A gas is held in a closed container and held at constant temperature. What is the effect of increasing the volume of the container by 3 times?

a. The pressure is tripled.
b. The pressure increases by one-third.
c. The pressure decreases to one-third.
d. The pressure remains constant.

104. Two cars driving in opposite directions collide. If you ignore friction and any other outside interactions, which of the following statements is always true?

a. The total momentum is conserved.
b. The sum of the potential and kinetic energy is conserved.
c. The total velocity of the cars is conserved.
d. The total impulse is conserved.

105. Which of the following is NOT true regarding exothermic and endothermic processes or reactions?

a. Exothermic reactions release heat energy.
b. The melting of ice is an endothermic process.
c. The burning of butane is an exothermic process.
d. The change in enthalpy is positive for an exothermic reaction.

106. In which taxonomic group are organisms MOST alike?

a. Phylum
b. Family
c. Class
d. Order

107. Which of the following animal structures is NOT paired to its correct function?

a. Muscle System – controls movement through three types of muscle tissue
b. Nervous System – controls sensory responses by carrying impulses away from and toward the cell body
c. Digestive System – breaks down food for absorption into the blood stream where it is delivered to cells for respiration
d. Circulatory System – exchanges gases with the environment by delivering oxygen to the bloodstream and releasing carbon dioxide

108. A population of pea plants has 25% dwarf plants and 75% tall plants. The tall allele, *T* is dominant to the dwarf allele, *t*. What is the frequency of the *T* allele?

a. 0.75
b. 0.67
c. 0.5
d. 0.25

109. Which of the following describes the correct short-term storage method for liquid-filled pH probes?

a. Store the pH probes in distilled water.
b. Store the pH probes on a dry shelf.
c. Store the pH probes in a potassium chloride solution.
d. Store the pH probes in hydrochloric acid.

110. Which of the following wastes may be suitable for sink or sewer disposal?

a. Acetic acid
b. Benzene
c. Acetone
d. Mercury

111. Heat is transmitted through solid materials via:

a. Conduction
b. Convection
c. Radiation
d. All three

112. Which of the following is Avogadro's number?

a. 2.063×10^{23}
b. 6.023×10^{22}
c. 6.022×10^{23}
d. 2.063×10^{22}

113. The moon plays an important role in which of the following earth events?

a. Tides
b. Earthquakes
c. Earth's orbit
d. Northern Lights

114. Which of the following is false regarding solar energy?

a. Solar energy is environmentally friendly
b. Solar energy has the greatest conversion efficiency
c. Solar energy is low maintenance
d. Solar energy is silent

115. What is the name of the process by which a bacterial cell splits into two new cells?

a. Mitosis
b. Meiosis
c. Replication
d. Binary fission

116. According to Coulomb's law of electric force, which of the following statements is true?

a. The force between two charged objects is directly proportional to the square of the distance between them.
b. The force between two charged objects is inversely related to the square of the distance between them.
c. The force between two charged objects is inversely related to the distance between them.
d. The force between two charged objects is inversely related to the square root of the distance between them.

117. Which of the following is an example of an absolute age?

a. A fossil is 37 million years old.
b. A rock is less than 100,000 years old.
c. An organic artifact is between 5,000 and 10,000 years old.
d. All of the above

118. During the process of oogenesis, primary oocytes produce:

a. Sperm
b. Eggs
c. Oogonia
d. Stem cells

119. When we look at a straw in a glass of water, the straw appears broken or bent at the waterline. This appearance is a function of:

a. Scattering
b. Absorption
c. Reflection
d. Refraction

120. Place the following in the correct order of increasing solubility in water.

a. Butanol < ethanol < octane < NaCl
b. Ethanol < NaCl < octane < butanol
c. NaCl < octane < butanol < ethanol
d. Octane < butanol < ethanol < NaCl

121. Which of the following ideas most aligns with Darwin's work in *On the Origin of Species*?

a. If an organism changes during its life in order to adapt to its environment, those changes are passed on to its offspring.
b. The geological processes that alter the earth are uniform through time.
c. Human populations will rapidly increase unless kept in check by limits in food supply.
d. Nature selects the best-adapted varieties to survive and reproduce.

122. The brain is part of the:

a. Integumentary system
b. Nervous system
c. Endocrine system
d. Respiratory system

123. You are watching the Olympic ice skating championships and see the pairs are up next. They begin their routine facing each other with their palms up and against each other. When the music starts, they push themselves apart with their palms. What type of force is this?

a. Magnetic
b. Balanced
c. Action and reaction force
d. Centripetal force

124. The year-round warmth of tropical rainforests is best explained by:

a. Their proximity to warm ocean currents
b. The forest canopy's ability to trap heat
c. The high humidity caused by frequent rainfall
d. Regular, intense solar energy

125. The major advantage of sexual reproduction over asexual forms is that

a. it allows for rapid colonization of new habitats.
b. it promotes genetic diversity.
c. it produces more offspring.
d. it involves chromosomes.

126. Which of the following characteristics is consistent with an acid?

a. Turns litmus paper blue
b. Accepts a proton
c. Reacts with zinc to produce hydrogen gas
d. Produces OH^- ions in aqueous solutions

127. Which of the following correctly describes the impact science has had on HIV?

a. HIV has been eradicated by vaccinations of inactivated HIV.
b. The progression from HIV to AIDS can be controlled by antiretroviral drugs.
c. HIV can be cured by antiretroviral drugs.
d. HIV mutations have been prevented by antiretroviral drugs.

128. When metamorphic rock is stressed unevenly during recrystallization, it can result in:

a. Foliation
b. Contact metamorphism
c. Regional metamorphism
d. Extrusion

129. Which of the following statements correctly describes a difference between the lithosphere and the asthenosphere?

a. The asthenosphere is composed of atmospheric gas, while the lithosphere is composed of liquids and solids.
b. The asthenosphere is hotter and more fluid than the lithosphere.
c. The lithosphere is hotter and has a different chemical composition than the asthenosphere.
d. Heat is transferred through conduction in the asthenosphere, while it is transferred through convection in the lithosphere.

130. Which part of a hurricane features the strongest winds and greatest rainfall?

a. Eye wall
b. Front
c. Eye
d. Outward spiral

131. Which of the following is responsible for the passage of water through a plant?

a. Cohesion
b. Adhesion
c. Osmosis
d. Transpiration

132. Of the following life forms, which has a life cycle featuring an incomplete metamorphosis?

a. Butterflies
b. Dragonflies
c. Amphibians
d. Mammals

133. What characteristic of electromagnetic radiation determines if it is classified as a radio wave or an x-ray?

a. Intensity
b. Phase angle
c. Wavelength
d. Speed of light

134. You blow up a rubber balloon and hold the opening tight with your fingers. You then release your fingers, causing air to blow out of the balloon. This pushes the balloon forward, causing the balloon to shoot across the room. Which of Newton's laws best explains the cause of this motion?

a. Newton's First Law
b. Newton's Second Law
c. Newton's Third Law
d. Newton's Fourth Law

135. In a pond, eutrophication, the pollution of water by plant nutrients, can occur, causing chemical, biological, and ecological changes to the pond. As plant material begins to decompose and carbon dioxide begins to increase, what would happen to the fish in the pond?

a. They would flourish
b. They would relocate to another area
c. They would die off
d. They would not be affected

136. A uranium isotope is represented by the symbol $^{238}_{92}U$. How many neutrons does an atom of this isotope contain?

a. 92
b. 330
c. 238
d. 146

137. A space station is revolving in a circular orbit around Earth. Consider the following three statements:

I. The center of mass of the space station is necessarily located at its geometric center.
II. The center of mass is moving at a constant velocity.
III. The center of mass of the space station is moving at a constant speed.

Which of the following statements is true?

a. I is true.
b. II is true.
c. III is true.
d. I, II, and III are not true.

138. Before they can be used by the body as fuel, complex carbohydrates must be converted into:

a. Glucose
b. Amino acids
c. Lipids
d. Folic acid

139. Most organic molecules have all of the following properties EXCEPT:

a. High solubility in water
b. A low melting point
c. Covalent bonds
d. High flammability

Refer to the following for questions 140–141:

The planet's oceans are experiencing climate changes, pollution, and overfishing. In some areas, zones that would normally host abundant aquatic life are now considered "dead zones."

140. Which of the following causes of ocean destruction is not a result of human activity?

a. Diminishment of coral reefs
b. Destruction of food webs
c. Tectonic plate shift
d. Degradation or total loss of wetlands

141. The main human-caused reason for these "dead zones" is:

a. Evaporation
b. Invasive species
c. Use of chemical fertilizers
d. Global warming

142. When heat is removed from water during condensation, which of the following are formed.

a. Atoms
b. Covalent bonds
c. Intermolecular bonds
d. Ionic bonds

143. Which of the following historical figures is NOT correctly matched with his contribution to modern science?

a. Louis Pasteur and the germ concept of disease
b. Thomas Edison and the theory of relativity
c. Johannes Kepler and the laws of planetary motion
d. Nicolaus Copernicus and the heliocentric view of the solar system

144. Which of the following is an example of a trace fossil?

a. A mouse jaw
b. A footprint
c. A shark tooth
d. A cast of a skull

145. Which of the following is the most immediate effect of acid rain?

a. Loss of fish due to toxicity of water
b. Disease- and pest-ridden forest trees
c. Unwanted algae growth where a river enters the ocean
d. Deterioration of buildings and monuments

146. Place the following elements in order of decreasing electronegativity:

N, As, Bi, P, Sb

a. As > Bi > N > P > Sb
b. N > P > As > Sb > Bi
c. Bi > Sb > As > P > N
d. P > N > As > Sb > Bi

147. Which of these refers to the oceans and water areas of Earth?

a. Atmosphere
b. Hydrosphere
c. Exosphere
d. Lithosphere

148. All living things have:

a. Organelles
b. Cells
c. Tissues
d. Cell walls

149. A substance has a half-life of 2.4×10^4 years. How long does it take for 87.5% of the substance to decay?

a. 2.1×10^4 years
b. 4.5×10^4 years
c. 7.2×10^4 years
d. 9.6×10^4 years

150. Which of the following conclusions can be drawn from the data presented in the graph below?

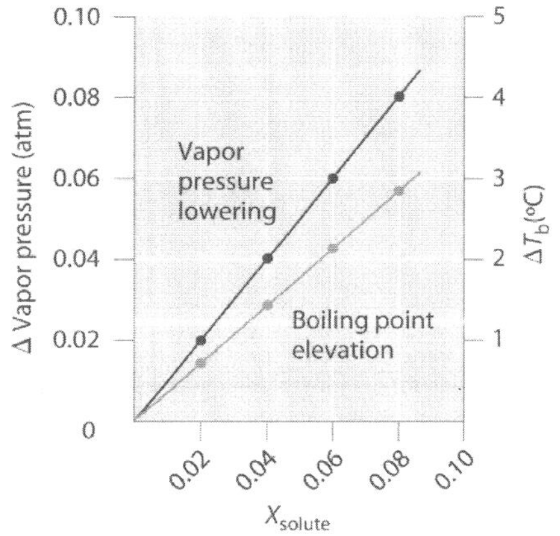

a. Increasing the solute increases the vapor pressure and decreases the boiling point of this solution.
b. Increasing the solute increases the vapor pressure and increases the boiling point of this solution.
c. Increasing the solute decreases the vapor pressure and decreases the boiling point of this solution.
d. Increasing the solute decreases the vapor pressure and increases the boiling point of this solution.

151. Which of the following is NOT a correct statement about plants?

a. Plants have different cell structures from animals.
b. Most plants primarily obtain energy from sunlight.
c. Plants do not produce sexually.
d. The green pigment in many plants is called chlorophyll.

152. Adding a catalyst to a reaction will do which of the following?

a. Shift the reaction equilibrium towards the products
b. Increase the temperature of the reaction
c. Decrease the energy of activation for the reaction
d. Increase the purity of the reaction products

153. Which of the following is a negative impact of reservoirs or dams?

a. Higher likelihood of flooding
b. Decreased dissolved oxygen
c. Increased rate of soil erosion
d. Less protection of water from pollution

154. Which of the following plant hormones is most likely to delay aging when sprayed on cut flowers and fruit?

a. Ethylene
b. Gibberellins
c. Cytokinins
d. Abscisic acid

155. A guyot is defined as:

a. Any undersea mountain more than 1,000 meters high
b. A seamount with a flattened top
c. An undersea mountain chain
d. A trough in the ocean floor

156. 1 mole of water and 1 mole of argon are in a cylinder at 110 °C and 1 atm of pressure. The temperature of the cylinder is reduced to –5 °C. Which statement about the contents of the cylinder is most accurate?

a. The pressure in the cylinder is decreased, and the partial pressure of argon is less than that of water.
b. The pressure in the cylinder is about the same, and the partial pressure of water is less than that of argon.
c. The pressure in the cylinder is decreased, and the partial pressure of water is much less than that of argon.
d. The pressure in the cylinder is decreased, and the partial pressure of water is the same as argon.

157. The most severe mass extinction event in Earth's history was the:

a. Cretaceous-Tertiary Event
b. Permian-Triassic Event
c. Ordovician-Silurian Event
d. Late Devonian Event

158. What is primary driving force in the development a hurricane?

a. High winds
b. Ocean temperatures
c. Cloud cover
d. Contact with land

159. The energy flow through an ecosystem is represented by an energy pyramid. In the energy pyramid for a terrestrial ecosystem, the producers utilize 6,000 kilocalories per square meter per year. What approximate amount of energy is transferred to the third trophic level of this ecosystem?

a. 0.6 kilocalories per square meter per year
b. 6 kilocalories per square meter per year
c. 60 kilocalories per square meter per year
d. 600 kilocalories per square meter per year

160. Which biome is most likely to support the growth of epiphytes?

a. Deserts
b. Tropical rain forests
c. Temperate deciduous forests
d. Taigas

Answer Key and Explanations for Test #2

1. C: When fault-block mountains such as those in the Western United States are formed, sections that are lifted by tensional forces are called horsts. Blocks that are lowered in elevation are called grabens. The term "rift" refers to the entire area that is affected by the separation of a continental plate.

2. C: The chaparral biome features scrubby plants and small evergreen trees and also has a hot, dry summer followed by a wetter winter. This biome is mainly found around the Mediterranean Sea, though there are also chaparrals in Australia, South Africa, and the American Southwest. The taiga is a colder biome found primarily in northern Europe and Asia. The vegetation of the taiga is mainly scattered stands of coniferous trees. A coniferous forest, meanwhile, is a warmer forest composed of trees that have needles and cones rather than leaves. These trees are better suited for a cold climate than are deciduous trees. A savanna is a tropical grassland with only a few trees. Savannas are clustered around the equator.

3. A: Vultures eat carrion, or dead animals, so they are considered scavengers. Detritivores are heterotrophs that eat decomposing organic matter such as leaf litter. They are usually small.

4. B: A longer life span does not necessarily lead to more productive years. It also leads to a larger aged population and increases the rate of population growth. Re-examining moral beliefs is not necessarily a drawback. New diseases may arise but medical advances may aid in the cure of these diseases.

5. B: Venus experiences a greenhouse effect similar to that observed on Earth as its dense atmosphere traps the solar radiation and creates a greenhouse effect. The greenhouse gases, including ozone, carbon dioxide, water vapor, and methane, trap infrared radiation that is reflected back toward the atmosphere. While both Venus and Earth experience the greenhouse effect, Venus's greenhouse effect is much more severe. Earth, on the other hand, has many more natural convective processes that help move carbon and other gases around, tempering the effect some. Human activity produces byproducts that contribute to the greenhouse effect. Some practices that increase the amount of greenhouse gases are burning natural gas and oil; farming, which leads to more methane and nitrous oxide; deforestation, which decreases the amount of offset oxygen; and population growth in general, which increases the volume of greenhouse gases. Increased gases mean more infrared radiation is trapped. While the greenhouse effect is not itself debated, the long-term effects tend to be hotly debated among scientists and in political agendas.

6. C: The ideal mechanical advantage of a simple machine is determined by the ratio of input distance to output distance. Since the input distance is 1.5 m and the output distance is 0.5 m, the ideal mechanical advantage for this pulley is 3.

7. B: Density-dependent limiting factors on population growth are factors that vary with population density. Pollution from a factory, volcanic eruptions, frosts, and fires do not vary as a function of population size. Waste products, however, increase with population density and could limit further population increases.

8. B: The Biological Species Concept (BSC) states that the status of "species" is based on the natural reproductive isolation of populations. Populations that could potentially interbreed and produce fertile offspring but do not do so in nature are considered different species under the BSC. This species concept does not consider the ability to interbreed under artificial conditions: if two groups do not breed with one another for any reason (in nature), they are reproductively isolated and therefore different species according to the BSC. The isolation may be due to geography, behavior, appearance, or other factors. For example, the Eastern and Western meadowlark look very similar and have overlapping territories, but they have different songs. Individual meadowlarks identify others by their songs and only breed with those with the same song. Because the two populations are reproductively isolated from one another, they are considered different species under the BSC. If individuals with different songs did interbreed and produce fertile offspring, they would be considered the same species.

9. D: Mercury is a fat-soluble pollutant and can be stored in body tissues. Animals higher up the food chain, which eat other animals, are most likely to accumulate mercury in their bodies.

10. D: Air masses are named for the areas over which they form. Since maritime polar air masses form over oceans in frigid regions, they bring cold, moist weather. Since maritime tropical air masses form over oceans in warmer regions, they bring warm, moist weather. Since continental polar air masses form over northern Canada or Alaska, they bring cold, dry weather. Since continental tropical air masses form over deserts, they bring warm, dry weather.

11. D: Nonvascular plants do not produce seeds like angiosperms and gymnosperms do. They generally reproduce sexually, but produce spores instead of seeds.

12. C: Heat transfer can never occur from a cooler object to a warmer object. While the second law of thermodynamics implies that heat never spontaneously transfers from a cooler object to a warmer object, it is possible for heat to be transferred to a warmer object, given the proper input of work to the system. This is the principle by which a refrigerator operates. Work is done to the system to transfer heat from the objects inside the refrigerator to the air surrounding the refrigerator. All other answer choices are true.

13. D: For a general reaction, $aA + bB \rightarrow cC + dD$, the equilibrium equation would take the form:

$$\mathrm{K_{eq}} = \frac{[C]^c[D]^d}{[A]^a[B]^b}$$

where a, b, c, and d are the coefficients from the balanced chemical reaction. Pure liquids and solids are excluded from the equation. Since all reactants and products in the problem are gaseous, the equilibrium equation for the reaction would be:

$$\mathrm{K_{eq}} = \frac{[\mathrm{CCl_4}][\mathrm{HCl}]^4}{[\mathrm{CH_4}][\mathrm{Cl_2}]^4}$$

14. A: Repeating a measurement several times can increase the precision of the measurement. Calibrating the equipment should only be done once for a whole set of measurements. Calibrating for each use will add a source of error and prevent measurements from being able to be compared. None of the other choices are useful strategies to increase the precision of a measurement.

15. C: Sunlight consists of electromagnetic radiation in the form of photons. Sunlight is produced when hydrogen nuclei fuse to form helium. This nuclear reaction is called fusion. Fission occurs when a nucleus disintegrates into two smaller nuclei. In both fission and fusion, energy is released because the binding energy per nucleon increases. This decreases the mass of the nuclei.

16. C: Fossils are least likely to be found in igneous rock. Igneous rock is formed by extreme heat as magma escapes through the Earth's crust and cools. The remains of plants and animals in fossil form are not usually preserved under these conditions. Sedimentary rock (A) is where most fossils are found. Sedimentary rock is formed more slowly and is very abundant. Since soft mud and silts compress into layers, organisms can also be deposited. Metamorphic rock (B) is rock that has undergone change by heat and pressure. This usually destroys any fossils, but occasionally fossil remains are simply distorted and can be found in metamorphic rock.

17. B: The newton can be defined in terms of the fundamental units of meters, kilograms, and seconds as $\mathrm{N} = \mathrm{kg} \times \mathrm{m/s^2}$, so it is not a fundamental unit. Statement II is a result of $F = ma$, Newton's second law, which is true. If $F = 0\ \mathrm{N}$, then the acceleration is $0\ \mathrm{m/s^2}$. If the acceleration is $0\ \mathrm{m/s^2}$, then the speed is $0\ \mathrm{m/s}$ or a nonzero constant. This is a nonverbal statement of Newton's first law, meaning Newton's first law can be derived from his second law. Newton's second law cannot be derived from the universal law of gravity.

18. B: The Cambrian explosion occurred during the Cambrian Period in the Paleozoic Era, approximately 541,000,000 years ago. The Jurassic Period, known for the first giant dinosaurs, occurred during the Mesozoic Era and began approximately 201,000,000 years ago.

19. C: John Dalton proposed the atomic theory of matter in 1803. He stated that each element consists of tiny, indivisible particles called atoms. He did not believe that an atom could be further broken down.

20. C: Finches with beaks well-suited for the types of food available on an island had an evolutionary advantage. As a result, these finches survived and reproduced, a phenomenon known as natural selection. The finches share a common ancestor, regardless of the island on which they now live. Genetic drift refers to genetic changes that occur due to random chance; this would not account for different beaks on different islands. Introduction by humans would not account for different beaks, since phenotypes change over time.

21. D: Species may theoretically be able to inhabit a particular area, called its fundamental niche. But the presence of competing species may mean that it only occupies part of its niche, called a realized niche.

22. C: Because there are 2 moles of gas on the reactant side and 1 mole of gas on the product side, a pressure increase will increase the forward reaction rate force the reaction to go further to the right. This, in turn, lowers gas pressure to restore equilibrium. Reaction order is not affected by environment changes.

23. A: This is an issue that would be regulated by the Food and Drug Administration (FDA), as it regulates the packaging of meat products, among many other types of food. Answer B would not be an issue for the FDA. The Environmental Protection Agency (EPA) regulates issues regarding the environment as well as Superfund cleanups. Neither answer C, about genetic engineering of humans, nor answer D, about cell use in industry, relate to food and drugs and would not fall under the jurisdiction of the FDA.

24. C: Hydrogen bonds are a special type of dipole-dipole interaction between molecules that causes a strong attraction (negative dipole to positive dipole). This interaction gives water such a high surface tension that some small organisms, such as water striders, can move across its surface. Although water molecules are polar, they do not attract non-polar molecules, such as fats or oils. Thus, choice A is incorrect. Solid water is less dense than liquid water, which is why ice floats in water and why choice B is incorrect. Choice D is incorrect because water is generally a very good solvent, especially for substances whose molecules have polar or ionic bonds. Choice E is incorrect because water cannot produce more of either H^+ or OH^-, since both would be made in equal amounts from H_2O, making it a terrible buffer.

25. C: Alternation of generations means the alternation between the diploid and haploid phases in plants.

26. D: Gravitational collapse and high-energy collisions are both proposed explanations for the formation of black holes. Gravitational collapse occurs when the outward pressure exerted by an object is too weak to resist that object's own gravity. Collisions that produce conditions of sufficient density could also, in theory, create black holes. The accretion of matter is considered observational evidence for the existence of black holes.

27. C: Plants do not require nitrogen for photosynthesis. Plants need access to sunlight, carbon dioxide, and water to undergo photosynthesis. Carbon dioxide contains carbon (A) and oxygen (B), and water contains hydrogen (D) and oxygen (B).

28. D: Prolonging the life of individuals in a current population will lead to an older age composition. An increased birth rate will cause population growth, but a greater proportion will be younger, not older.

29. D: The ovary houses the ovules in a flower. Pollen grains fertilize ovules to create seeds, and the ovary matures into a fruit.

30. A: The central, supporting pillar of the tree is known as heartwood. Heartwood does not function in the transport of water, and even though it is dead, it will not decay or lose strength as long as the outer layers remain intact.

31. A: Chemical composition is not one of the physical properties used to classify minerals. The five major physical properties used to classify minerals are luster, hardness, cleavage, streak, and form. There is a separate classification system based on the chemical composition of minerals.

32. D: Expansion in the redshifts of galaxies, measurements of cosmic microwave background radiation, and measurements of the distribution of quasars and galaxies are all considered observational evidence in support of the Big Bang Theory. The abundance of certain "primordial elements" is also consistent with the theory.

33. B: Electrons, protons, and neutrons are subatomic particles. Electrons have the smallest mass. Protons and neutrons, which are nearly equal in mass, are several orders of magnitude more massive than electrons. Quarks are believed to be the components of protons and neutrons; while a quark has less mass than a complete proton or neutron, it still has more mass than an electron.

34. B: Stomata are the pores of the plant that open to release water via transpiration or close during adverse conditions like a drought to prevent the plant from dehydration. Stomata are flanked by guard cells that can respond to stimuli and regulate opening and closing. Pith refers to the central, spongy part of the stem in vascular plants. Sepals are modified leave that protect the flower bud before it opens.

35. B: Work is defined as the force used to move a mass over a distance. The amount of energy used to accomplish a job is a non-scientific definition of work. The amount of energy used per unit of time is the definition of power. Energy stored in an object due to its position is the definition of potential energy.

36. A: The prevailing westerlies drive weather systems to move west to east in the mid-latitudes. The direction refers to that which the wind is coming from. The polar easterlies that travel from the northeast occur between 90-60 degrees north latitude. The ones from the southeast are between 90-60 degrees south latitude. The trade winds refer to those occurring near the equator in the tropics moving east. The doldrums are also in the tropics, but they refer to an area of low-pressure where frequently the winds are light and unpredictable.

37. C: James Hutton is best known for proposing the theory of uniformitarianism. This geological theory, which is essentially the opposite of catastrophism, suggests that the laws and forces acting on the Earth have remained basically the same since the beginning of geologic time.

38. D: Respiration produces carbon dioxide and water. The net equation of respiration is the reverse of the equation for photosynthesis. Respiration is a series of reactions that consume glucose and oxygen to release energy and produce carbon dioxide and water. Oxygen and glucose are the substances that are broken down in respiration.

39. B: Biodiversity deals with living organisms and their interconnections within an environment. We know that the local pond is the best environment in which to observe a contained ecosystem. Gas-powered boats leave harmful chemicals in the pond water, which will be absorbed into the ground and by animals living in and around the water. Those animals will be contaminated with those chemicals, as will plants growing from the groundwater. By eliminating these chemical contaminants, the protected pond environment will host healthy and thriving species for many years to come.

40. A: The addition of energy causes a phase change. Phase changes are physical changes, not chemical changes. While sublimation is an example of a phase change, it occurs when a solid turns directly into a gas without passing through the liquid state. Condensation, another phase change, occurs when a gas turns to liquid.

41. A: Homeostasis is the process whereby an organism maintains the constant internal conditions necessary for life. Dynamic equilibrium must be maintained even as external conditions continually change. Metabolism refers to the combined chemical processes within a living cell or organism that are necessary for maintaining life. Respiration refers to the process by which cells derive energy from organic molecules. Symbiosis refers to a close association of two dissimilar species that is usually beneficial to one or both of the organisms.

42. B: A moving electron produces a circular magnetic field that is perpendicular to the velocity of the particle. Since the magnetic field produced by the electron exerts a magnetic force towards the electron, the charge on the particle is positive. This conclusion requires the correct application of the right-hand rule for the creation of a magnetic field by a current (thumb in the direction of the velocity of a positive charge with fingers curling in the direction of the magnetic field) and the right-hand rule for the magnetic force on a moving charge (fingers in the direction of the positively charged particle's velocity, thumb in the direction of the magnetic force, and palm in the direction of the magnetic field). Answer D is wrong because there are no particles with only a north pole or a south pole. There may be a force between the electron and the particle if the particle is a tiny magnet, but the direction of the force would depend on the magnet's orientation, and hence answer A is wrong.

43. D: The disposal of unused zygotes or embryos, and even the multiple embryos lost through successive unsuccessful implants, is an issue to those who believe life begins at conception. If life begins at conception, then regulations covering experimentation on human beings should be followed.

44. B: A volcano that is thought to be dormant is expected to erupt some time again in the future, but danger is not imminent. Dormant volcanoes are expected to erupt again in the future because they still show signs of internal volcanic activity. Extinct volcanoes are not expected to erupt again because they show no signs of activity. Active volcanoes are either erupting or about to erupt.

45. A: Observation includes collecting evidence, using the five senses, and writing descriptions. Classifying includes grouping items based on similarities, differences, and interrelationships. Inferring includes explaining or interpreting collected evidence. Communication is reporting to others what has been found by experimentation.

46. C: As the amplitude of the pendulum increases due to resonance, it will swing higher. However, the period of a pendulum is not connected to how high it swings. Only the length of the pendulum affects its period. The length of a pendulum will not be affected by how high it's swinging or whether it's in resonance.

47. C: Magnets do not have to be touching to attract or repel materials; they are able to do this from a distance. However, magnets do NOT work beyond their magnetic fields (D): the magnetic field is defined as the effective range or area of a magnet, so magnets only work within their magnetic fields by definition. Opposite poles of magnets do NOT repel (A), but instead attract each other. Conversely, the like poles of magnets do NOT attract (B), but instead repel one another.

48. D: The muscular system includes muscles, which allow a person's body to move. The integumentary system (A) includes organs such as the skin. While injuries to the skin can limit a person's range of movement, it does not enable movement. The digestive system (B) allows a person to eat and digest food, but does not allow a person to move. The endocrine system (C) is related to hormones, not a person's ability to move.

49. A: The higher the temperature of the liquid, the greater the solubility of the solid, while the higher the temperature, the lower the solubility of the gas.

50. A: Cardiac output is total volume of blood that is pumped by the heart over a certain period of time. This value is typically reported in the amount of liters per minute. Cardiac output is determined by the product of heart rate and stroke volume. Heart rate is the number of heartbeats per minute, and stroke volume is the amount of blood that is pumped by the left ventricle in each heartbeat or contraction. A typical heart can pump approximately 5 liters of blood per minute. As the intensity of exercise increases, the cardiac output can increase to as high as 40 liters per minute. An individual's heart rate will increase linearly until the maximum level is reached. Stroke volume, however, tends to increase to approximately 40-50% of the maximum and will then level off. Aerobic exercise helps to strengthen the heart, pump blood more efficiently, and increase stroke volume.

51. B: The freezing point of sea water is lower than that of fresh water as sea water is denser. It is denser because it has more dissolved salts. The freezing point changes with salinity, pressure, and density, but can be as low as –2 °C (28.4 °F), compared with 0 °C (32 °F) for fresh water.

52. B: Phosphorus is in the third period, so the outermost levels must be $3s$, $3p$. Phosphorus is in Group 5A, which indicates that it has 5 valence electrons. To fill the $3s$ and $3p$, 2 electrons first fill the s orbital, and then the remaining 3 electrons enter the p orbitals, making $3s^2 3p^3$.

53. D: Natural selection was Darwin's idea, not Lamarck's. Mendel discovered that genes are the basic units of inheritance. Lamarck's observation about use and disuse is true, although he did not connect it with the underlying mechanism of natural selection.

54. D: When the electrons are strongly bound to the atoms of a substance, these atoms seldom release their electrons and thus do not conduct electricity well; such materials are electrical insulators (e.g., air, wood, glass, plastic, cotton, and ceramics). Metals and other substances whose atoms have free electrons that can separate from the atoms and move about are electrical conductors; electrical current flows freely through materials with loose electrons.

55. D: Digestion of food in the small intestine occurs by bile secreted by the liver. This is a chemical change.

56. D: Living organisms change their behaviors according to internal cues, such as hunger, thirst, need for sunlight, need to reproduce, etc., and external cues like environmental changes, such as changes in temperature, amounts of water, availability of nutrients, etc. Their behavior is shaped NOT primarily by one or the other of these (A, B) but by both. It is not controlled solely by genetic programming (C), but it consists of adaptations to intrinsic needs and extrinsic changes in the environment.

57. D: It is true that the ocean's salinity is usually between 34 and 35 parts per thousand, or 35,000 parts per million. Oceans comprise about 70.8% of the Earth's surface, and the ocean's deepest point is over 10,000 meters below sea level. The Mediterranean is considered a sea, not an ocean.

58. B: Ohm's Law states that voltage and current in an electrical circuit are directly proportional to one another. Ohm's Law can be expressed as $V = IR$, where V is voltage, I is current and R is resistance. Voltage is also known as electrical potential difference and is the force that moves electrons through a circuit. For a given amount of resistance, an increase in voltage will result in an increase in current. Resistance and current are inversely proportional to each other. For a given voltage, an increase in resistance will result in a decrease in current.

59. B: Technology often results from scientific discoveries. The relationship between science and technology is evident when scientific discoveries prompt technologic advances.

60. A: Meiosis is a process that cuts the number of chromosomes per cell is cut in half. In animals, meiosis results in the formation of gametes, while in other organisms it results in spores.

61. C: In the field of geology, the term "uniformitarianism" refers to the belief that the natural forces, laws, and processes that shape the Earth have remained relatively constant over geologic time. This belief contradicts catastrophism, which maintains that dramatic events have been the primary forces involved in shaping the Earth.

62. B: On the Celsius scale, water freezes at 0 °C and boils at 100 °C. On the Kelvin scale, water freezes at 273.15 K and boils at 373.15 K. Both the Celsius and Kelvin scales have exactly 100 degrees between the freezing and boiling points of water. Since water freezes at 32 °F and boils at 212 °F on the Fahrenheit scale, the Fahrenheit scale has 180 degrees between the freezing and boiling points of water.

63. A: Experiments are conducted in order to test a hypothesis. Collecting data (B), identifying a control state (C), and choosing variables (D) are steps in conducting an experiment designed to test a hypothesis.

64. B: The relationship between the clown fish and the sea anemone is an example of mutualism - because both organisms are benefitting from the relationship. The Clown fish gains the protection from the anemone while offering protection to the anemone from being eaten by a certain type of fish.

65. C: Covalent compounds are usually formed by the combination of two or more non-metallic elements with one another. In these compounds, atoms share electrons. Ionic compounds are most often formed between a metal and a nonmetal. Organic compounds are covalent compounds that contain carbon and hydrogen atoms. Some of the compounds formed by non-metallic elements are polar, but not all of them.

66. A: The magnitude of the temperature on the Fahrenheit scale is calculated using the mathematical expression $°\mathrm{F} = \frac{9}{5}°\mathrm{C} + 32$. At the boiling point of water, 100 °C, the temperature in Fahrenheit is calculated to be 212 °F. Kelvin (absolute temperature) is calculated using the mathematical expression $\mathrm{K} = °\mathrm{C} + 273$. At 100 °C, the temperature in Kelvin is 373 K. Thus, the order from least to greatest is 100 °C, 212 °F, 373 K.

67. C: Percent error is calculated by the following equation.

$$\text{Percent error} = \frac{\text{Experimental value} - \text{Theoretical value}}{\text{Theoretical value}} \times 100\%$$

$$\text{Percent error} = \frac{0.410 - 0.385}{0.385} \times 100\% = 6.49\%$$

The percent error for the students' specific heat of copper is 6.49%.

68. D: Isotopes are variations of an element that have different numbers of neutrons. The various isotopes of an element have the same numbers of protons and electrons. For example, carbon has three naturally occurring isotopes: carbon-12, carbon-13 and carbon-14 (which is radioactive). Isotopes of an element differ in mass number, which is the number of protons and neutrons added together, but have the same atomic number, or number of protons.

69. A: Homeostasis involves the balancing of many biochemical systems and processes. Several of them include buffers as a means of expanding the range of stable conditions. In this instance, part of blood pH maintenance is controlled with the carbonic acid, H_2CO_3, and bicarbonate ion, HCO_3^-, buffer. While water, even when neutral, has a small amount of hydronium ions $(H_3O)^+$and hydroxide ions, OH^-, present, they do not act as a buffer (B). Electroplating copper onto tin is a redox reaction (C). The lack of solubility of aluminum hydroxide does not make it a buffer (D).

70. C: The diagram represents an ecological pyramid. The letter A represents the producers, such as plants. The letter B represents the primary consumers usually herbivores. The letter C stands for the secondary consumers, the carnivores that feed on the herbivores. A coyote is a carnivore and would, therefore, be in this group and represented by the letter C. The pyramid's fourth level, represented by a D, includes the decomposers, such as bacteria and fungi, which decompose dead organic material.

71. C: In a positive feedback loop, an action intensifies a chain of events that, in turn, intensify the conditions that caused the action beyond normal limits. Nursing stimulates lactation, which promotes nursing. Contractions during childbirth and sexual orgasm are examples of positive feedback.

72. D: A volcano occurs when a dike (a vertical fracture in the Earth's crust that fills with magma) reaches the Earth's surface and a plume (a spurt of magma) passes through it. Batholiths are large masses of igneous rock that form beneath the Earth's surface, and a sill is a horizontal fracture in the Earth's crust that fills with magma. When an oceanic plate is subducted by a continental plate, it results in the formation of mountain ranges and volcanic arcs.

73. C: In an ecosystem, when one species is affected by overfishing or pollution, other species will either thrive due to a lack of competition or become extinct for the same reasons. The question states that the other species were not impacted by the overfishing or pollution. Thus, their populations would not have decreased for those reasons. Once extinct, the other species were no longer the potential prey of the Blue Pike or competing against them for similar food sources and so had the opportunity to increase their population numbers.

74. C: The Gulf Stream, which is a surface current that originates in the Gulf of Mexico and travels across the Atlantic Ocean, makes the climate of Northern Europe warmer. After traveling up the eastern coast of the US, the Gulf Stream splits into two forks. The North Atlantic Drift travels across the ocean to warm Europe, while the southern fork travels toward West Africa.

75. B: An iron bar moving inside a coil of wire that contains a current would create an electromagnet. Rapidly spinning and rotating electrons inside an iron bar (A) creates a magnetic field. The movement of electrons through a complete circuit (C) is an electric current. Convection currents within the liquid core of Earth's interior (D) create the Earth's magnetic field.

76. D: Water is likely to have the shortest residence time in the atmosphere. Water molecules linger in the atmosphere for an estimated 9 days, while their residence time in glaciers may range from 20 to 100 years. Water molecules reside in lakes for approximately 50 to 100 years, and they stay in rivers for two to six months.

77. A: New species due to geographic isolation. Allopatric speciation refers to a new species brought about by geographic isolation. Speciation in general refers to the formation of a new species. Geographic isolation can be because of a great physical barrier or insurmountable distance between groups of individuals. This rules out Answer B, New species due to geographic overlap. Answer C, Hybrid species due to geographic overlap, is incorrect, as hybrid species has many definitions that do not necessarily relate to geography. Answer D, Loss of diversity of a species due to geographic divergence, is also incorrect as it does not refer to loss of diversity.

78. D: Vinegar is a 5% solution of acetic acid. The pH scale ranges from 0 to 14. Substances with a pH near zero are strong acids, and substances with a pH near 14 are strong bases. Substances with a pH of 7 are neutral. Bleach is a strong base, and ammonia is a relatively weak base. Water is neutral. Since vinegar is the only acid listed, the pH of vinegar is the closest to a pH of 1.

79. B: The synaptonemal complex is a multi-protein complex that serves to line up and connect homologous chromatids during prophase of meiosis I. It facilitates the exchange of genetic material between non-sister chromatids (i.e., crossing over) by ensuring that the chromatids are perfectly aligned and exchange equivalent segments. It is often described as a "molecular zipper." The points at which the homologous chromatids cross one another to exchange genetic material are known as chiasmata (singular: chiasma). The synaptonemal complex is disassembled once the crossovers have resolved, at which point prophase of meiosis I is complete.

80. B: Answer B correctly states the definition of a conductor. Answer C is incorrect because a current will also flow in an insulator, for example, although that current will be very low. In metals, the current flow caused by an electric field is much greater than in an insulator or semiconductor because the electrons are not bound to any particular atom, but are free to move. Answer D is incorrect because a vacuum tube is a device that electrons can flow in, but a vacuum tube is not considered a conductor.

81. B: Acids and bases will react violently if accidentally mixed, as will reducing and oxidizing agents. Both reactions can be highly exothermic and uncontrollable.

82. C: Physical weathering of rocks can be caused by changes in temperature and pressure, as well as the freezing and thawing of water on the surfaces of rocks. Oxidation is a chemical process, not a physical one. Therefore, it is considered an example of chemical rather than physical weathering.

83. C: Newton's first law of motion states that an object in motion will remain in motion at a constant velocity unless acted upon by an external force. This resistance to changes in motion, known as inertia, is why seatbelts are needed; without one a body would keep moving forward when decelerating. Newton's first law of motion is often referred to as the law of inertia.

84. A: While landfills are necessary, potential problems include soil contamination, surface water contamination, pollution, and leachate.

85. B: Negative beta emission represents the spontaneous decay of a neutron into a proton with the release of an electron. Therefore, the resulting nucleus will have one more proton than it did before the reaction, and protons represent the atomic number of an atom. Alpha decay results in the emission of a helium nucleus. The resulting nucleus of an alpha decay would lose two protons and two neutrons, causing a decrease in both the atomic number and the mass number. In contrast, positive beta (beta-plus) emission converts a proton into a neutron and thus decreases the atomic number by 1. Gamma decay does not affect the numbers of protons or neutrons in the nucleus. It is an emission of a photon, or packet of energy.

86. D: When adding, the answer should be rounded to the same number of decimal places as the measurement with the fewest decimal places. The total mass is obtained by adding up all four measurements. This yields 35.5918. Since the first and second masses are precise to only a hundredth of a gram, your answer can't be more precise than this. The number 35.5918, when rounded to two decimal places, is 35.59.

87. D: Of these options, the only real direct impact of climate change is the rising sea level. This is due to the melting glaciers and ice sheets. Also, the oceans expand slightly as they get warmer.

88. B: Flowers are the reproductive organs of a plant. Flowering plants reproduce by sexual reproduction where the gametes join to form seeds. Pollen is sperm. Pollinators help transfer the sperm to the ovule, by way of the stigma. The style is the part of the female reproduction system that transports the sperm between the stigma and the ovary, which are all parts of the pistil. The stigma is the sticky tip of the style on which the pollen lands. Sepals are usually small leaves between or underneath the petals and are not as obvious or as large and colorful as the petals.

89. C: 100 g of HBr equals 1.23 moles, and 100 g of Mg equals 4.11 moles. From the coefficients of the balanced equation, the ratio of HBr to Mg is 2 : 1. This means that to react 1.23 moles of HBr, 2.46 moles of Mg would be required. Since 4.11 moles of Mg are present, Mg is in excess.

90. B: Fission occurs when the nucleus breaks up into two smaller nuclei. When certain nuclear isotopes absorb a neutron, they become unstable and split, starting the process of fission. The average binding energy per nucleon increases with a fission reaction, and the two new nuclei are more stable than the initial nucleus. The increase in binding energy comes from the changes in mass of the protons and neutrons (note: both protons and neutrons are nucleons). The release of energy is part of the fission reaction, but this does not explain why the fission reaction occurs.

91. C: A parasite is an organism that feeds off the nutritional assets of another living thing called the host, which can lead to the host becoming malnourished or dying. Symbiosis occurs when there is a benefit to both organisms. A predator eats its prey. A producer produces food in the form of plant material that is eaten by a consumer.

92. C: Predictions of the solubility of each chemical at 150 degrees Celsius can be made by extending the lines or curves. Since the data for KBr is relatively linear, it is reasonable to assume that the solubility may increase to about 130 g per 100 g H_2O. If the curves for $NaClO_3$ and KNO_3 continue along the same lines, then these predictions are too low. The prediction for NaCl is too high.

93. B: Elements and compounds are both pure substances. Elements consist of only one type of atom. Compounds consist of more than one type of atom. Molecules may make up either elements or compounds. Mixtures are two or more substances that are physically combined but not chemically united.

94. B: A total solar eclipse can be observed only by viewers located within the umbra. The umbra is the darkest part of the shadow, and the light source is not visible from it. The penumbra is the lighter portion of the shadow from which the light source is partially visible. In a solar eclipse, the Moon passes between the Earth and the Sun, and viewers in the umbra experience a total solar eclipse.

95. C: In plants, all eggs and sperm are produced by gametophytes. In mosses, the gametophyte is the most prominent stage. In angiosperms, gametophytes are tiny and found inside anthers and pistils.

96. B: An occluded front occurs when a cold front has overtaken a warm front, resulting in a mature storm system. A stationary front does not move. A cold front brings cold air, while a warm front brings warm air.

97. A: A scientific theory is a dynamic set of ideas that attempts to explain a scientific phenomenon. Scientific theories are not proven fact. Scientific facts, or laws, are based in extensive evidence and concrete knowledge about our world and are widely accepted descriptions of an aspect of reality. Choice A lists a theory, the Big Bang, which refers to a set of ideas about the origin of the universe. The laws of motion are proven facts that explain the behavior of objects in our environment. Choices B and D both list sets of theories without facts. Choice C shows two scientifically accepted facts, those of mass and electricity conservation and the process of carbon-14 dating of objects.

98. C: The best control group would be women with wrinkles around their eyes using a cream that has no effect. A scientific control group is used to minimize the unintended influence of other variables on a scientific study. Such extraneous variables include researcher bias, environmental changes, and biological variation. Scientific controls ensure that data are valid and are a vital part of the scientific method.

99. C: One way to measure the density of an irregularly shaped object is to submerge it in water and measure the displacement. This is done by taking the mass (40 grams), then finding the volume by measuring how much water it displaces. Fill a graduated cylinder with water and record the amount. Put the object in the water and record the water level. Subtract the difference in water levels to get the amount of water displaced, which is also the volume of the object. In this case, 4.5

liters minus 2.5 liters equals 2 liters. Divide mass by volume (40 grams divided by 2 liters) to get 20 g/L (grams per liter).

100. A: Density is mass per volume, typically expressed in units such as g/cm^3, or kg/m^3.

101. D: The process whereby a radioactive element releases energy slowly over a long period of time to lower its energy and become more stable is best described as decay. The nucleus undergoing decay, known as the parent nuclide, spontaneously releases energy most commonly through the emission of an alpha particle, a beta particle, or a gamma ray. The changed nucleus, called the daughter nuclide, is now more stable than the parent nuclide, although the daughter nuclide may undergo another decay to an even more stable nucleus. A decay chain is a series of decays of a radioactive element into different elements.

102. A: A lysosome is an organelle that is thought to be linked to the aging process and contains digestive enzymes that break down food and unneeded substances. Chromatin is the structure created by DNA and various proteins in the cell's nucleus during interphase and condenses to form chromosomes. Plastids are found in plants and algae. They often contain pigments and usually help make chemical compounds for the plant. The Golgi apparatus prepares macromolecules like proteins and lipids for transport.

103. C: The pressure decreases to one-third. A gas in a closed container at constant temperature will decrease in pressure to one-third when the volume of the container is tripled. The ideal gas law is $PV = nRT$ where P is pressure, V is volume, n is the moles of the gas, R is the gas constant, and T is temperature. Dividing by volume gives the following expression for pressure:

$$P = \frac{nRT}{V}$$

Boyle's Law indicates that pressure and volume are inversely proportional. The pressure cannot be increased because that would imply that pressure and volume are directly proportional.

104. A: In a closed system (when you ignore outside interactions), the total momentum is constant and conserved. The total energy would also be conserved, although not the sum of the potential and kinetic energy. Some of the energy from the collision would be turned into thermal energy (heat) for example. Nor is the total velocity conserved, even though the velocity is a component of the momentum, since the momentum also depends on the mass of the cars. The impulse is a force over time that causes the momentum of a body to change. It doesn't make sense to think of impulse as conserved, since it's not necessarily constant throughout a collision.

105. D: Exothermic reactions release heat energy, while endothermic reactions absorb heat energy. Since the burning of butane releases heat energy, the reaction is exothermic. Since the melting of ice absorbs heat energy, the process is endothermic. Since an exothermic reaction releases heat energy, the change in enthalpy is negative.

106. B: Organisms that belong to the same taxonomic group of family are most alike. In biological taxonomy, the ranks in descending order are Domain, Kingdom, Phylum, Class, Order, Family, Genus, and Species. The ranks become more exclusive and specific as the classification descends. Phylum, class, and order are all higher than the family group. The higher the rank, the fewer requirements it takes to be a member. Two mnemonics for taxonomy are Dashing Kings Play Cards On Fat Green Stools or Dear King Philip Cuts Open Five Green Snakes.

107. D: The circulatory system and gas exchange with the environment is not paired correctly. It is the respiratory system that exchanges gases with the environment by delivering oxygen to the bloodstream and releasing carbon dioxide. The circulatory system transports nutrients, gases, hormones, and blood to and away from cells. The muscle system controls movement through three types of muscle tissue. The nervous system controls sensory responses by carrying impulses away from and toward the cell body. The digestive system breaks down food for absorption into the bloodstream where it is delivered to cells for respiration.

108. C: According to Hardy-Weinberg equilibrium, $p + q = 1$ and $p^2 + 2pq + q^2 = 1$. In this scenario, $q^2 = 0.25$, so $q = 0.5$, and p must also be 0.5.

109. C: The pH probes should be stored according to the manufacturer's instructions. In general, pH probes should never be stored in water or stored dry without first draining the electrode. They should always be stored in an appropriate buffer or reference electrolyte, which is usually a 3M – 4M potassium chloride solution.

110. A: If diluted, acetic acid may be disposed of by sink or sewer. Vinegar is a 5% acetic acid solution and is commonly used in the kitchen. In general, alkanoic acids with 5 or fewer carbon atoms, such as acetic acid, butyric acid, and formic acid, may be disposed of by sink or sewer. Chemicals such as benzene, acetone, and mercury should never be disposed of by sink or sewer.

111. A: Three ways of transmitting heat are conduction (A), convection (B), and radiation (C). When heat is transmitted through solids, this is done via conduction. Conduction occurs between solid materials directly contacting one another. Convection (B) is how heat travels through liquids and gases. Heat makes them expand, lowering their density so they rise. When they cool, they recover density and fall. This heating-rising and cooling-falling process creates a current known as convection. Radiation (C), like the heat from the sun, occurs when electromagnetic waves travel through space and transfer heat to objects, like the Earth, that they touch. Therefore, (D) is incorrect.

112. C: Avogadro's number is the number of particles in one mole of a substance. Avogadro's number is 6.022×10^{23}. One mole of any substance contains 6.022×10^{23} particles of that substance.

113. A: The moon's gravitational pull against the earth causes the earth's oceans to bulge out at the points nearest to and farthest from the moon, causing the displacement of water that occurs twice a day, known as high and low tide.

114. B: Pros of solar energy include the facts that it is renewable, abundant, environmentally friendly, low maintenance, and silent. Cons of solar energy include that it is expensive and intermittent and requires a lot of space. Solar panels require rare minerals like indium and tellurium and at this point are only about 20% efficient in harvesting energy—putting them behind several other alternative methods. Other solar harvesting methods besides the photoelectric effect include concentrated solar and water heating.

115. D: Binary fission is the process of a bacterial cell splitting into two new cells. Fission is a form of asexual reproduction in which an organism divides into two components; each of these two parts will develop into a distinct organism. The two cells, known as daughter cells, are identical. Mitosis, on the other hand, is the part of eukaryotic cell division in which the cell nucleus divides. In meiosis, the homologous chromosomes in a diploid cell separate, reducing the number of chromosomes in each cell by half. In replication, a cell creates duplicate copies of DNA.

116. B: Coulomb's law of electric force is represented by $F = k\frac{q_1 q_2}{d^2}$ in which F is the electrostatic force, k is a constant related to the medium between the charges, q_1 and q_2 are the strengths of the charges, and d is the distance between the charges. Since the square of the distance is in the denominator, the force is inversely related to the square of the distance between the charges.

117. A: When a fossil is determined to be 37 million years old, this is an example of an absolute age. Absolute dating, which can be accomplished through the use of radiometric techniques, establishes precise ages for materials, while stratigraphic techniques only produce relative dates. Relative dating can establish approximate ages for rocks and fossils based on clues in the surrounding rock, but it cannot be used to determine absolute age.

118. B: Oogenesis is the process that gives rise to the ovum, or egg, in mammals. The oocyte is the immature egg cell in the ovary. In humans, one oocyte matures during each menstrual cycle. It develops first into an intermediate form called the ootid, and eventually into an ovum. The prefix *oo-* is derived from Greek, and means "egg."

119. D: Refraction is the process whereby the speed of light is changed as it passes from one transparent medium, like air, to another, like water. The change in speed bends the light wave. Scattering (A) is the process whereby light bounces back at multiple angles when it strikes a rough or uneven surface (instead of bouncing back at a single angle as when it strikes a smooth surface). When light bounces back off a surface, this is reflection (C). Materials that do not reflect *any* light waves (smoothly or scattered) or refract any light waves appear opaque (i.e., we cannot see through them) because they take in all frequencies of light; this is absorption (B).

120. D: Octane is a nonpolar hydrocarbon with little or no water solubility. Butanol is an alcohol with a small amount of solubility due to its polar —OH group. Ethanol is a smaller, more polar alcohol that is very soluble in water. NaCl is an ionic salt that is highly soluble in water.

121. D: Darwin introduced his idea of natural selection in *On the Origin of Species*, in which he stated that nature selects the best-adapted varieties to survive and reproduce. Lamarck wrote *Philosophie Zoologique*, in which he proposed a theory of inheritance of acquired characteristics. This theory states that if an organism changes during its life to adapt to its environment, those changes are passed on to its offspring. Lyell wrote *Principles of Geology*, in which he introduced his idea of uniformitarianism, which states that the geological processes that alter the earth are uniform through time. Malthus wrote *An Essay on the Principle of Population*, in which he stated that human populations will rapidly increase unless kept in check by limits in food supply.

122. B: The brain is part of the nervous system.

123. C: The ice skaters are applying Newton's Third Law to create an equal and opposite reaction force, causing both partners to move. When one skater pushes on the other, the other pushes back with equal and opposite force.

124. D: Because tropical rainforests lie near the equator, they typically receive 12 hours of intense sunlight on a regular basis; as a result, they are typically warm year-round. None of the other options given describe the primary cause of the heat. Although a forest canopy might indeed help trap heat, for example, the canopy itself is not the actual source of the heat itself; this eliminates option (B). Similarly, although humidity might make the heat seem more intense (due to chemical properties of water), humidity itself is not the cause of heat. This eliminates choice (C). Option (A) can be rejected because it is the sun, not warm ocean currents, that are the principle cause of warmth in tropical rainforests.

125. B: Sexual reproduction allows the genetic information from two parents to mix. Recombination events between the two parental copies of individual genes may occur, creating new genes. The production of new genes and of new gene combinations leads to an increase in genetic diversity within the population, which is a great advantage in terms of adapting to changes in the environment.

126. C: Acids react with metals like zinc to produce hydrogen gas. Acids turn litmus red, not blue. Acids donate protons, they do not accept them. Acids produce H^+ ions in aqueous solution, not OH^- ions.

127. B: Currently, there is no vaccine and no cure for HIV. HIV continues to mutate and evolve unchecked; however, the progression from HIV to AIDS can be controlled by antiretroviral drugs.

128. A: When metamorphic rock is stressed unevenly during recrystallization, it can result in foliation. Foliation is characterized by banded rock, and it occurs when certain types of minerals are reoriented during recrystallization due to uneven shortening or compression of the rock.

129. B: It is true that the asthenosphere is hotter and more fluid than the lithosphere. The asthenosphere is a hot, ductile layer within the upper mantle upon which the lithosphere, or the uppermost mantle and Earth's crust, is situated. Heat is transferred within the asthenosphere through a process called convection, which sometimes causes movement in the tectonic plates that make up the lithosphere.

130. A: The eye wall of a hurricane has the strongest winds and the greatest rainfall. The eye wall is the tower-like rim of the eye. It is from this wall that clouds extend out, which are seen from above as the classic outward spiral pattern. A hurricane front is the outermost edge of its influence; although there will be heavy winds and rain in this area, the intensity will be relatively small. The eye of a hurricane is actually a place of surprising peace. In this area, dry and cool air rushes down to the ground or sea. Once there, the air is caught up in the winds of the eye wall and is driven outward at a furious pace.

131. D: *Transpiration* is the primary process responsible for the bulk passage of water through a plant. It describes the evaporation of water from the leaves, which causes negative pressure that pulls water upward from the roots. Cohesion, adhesion, and osmosis all support this process. *Cohesion* is the attractive force between two molecules of the same substance. *Adhesion* is the attractive force between molecules of different substances. *Osmosis* is a process in which water diffuses through a selectively permeable membrane.

132. B: Certain primitive insects, including dragonflies, grasshoppers, and cockroaches, undergo an incomplete metamorphosis in their life cycle. A metamorphosis is a change in form. In insects, a complete metamorphosis, as butterflies (A) undergo, includes the stages of egg, larva, pupa (called a chrysalis in butterflies), and imago, the adult form. An incomplete metamorphosis in insects includes an egg, nymph, and adult stage, but no pupa. Amphibians (C), like frogs, toads, and newts, undergo complete metamorphoses. For example, frogs go from eggs to tadpoles living underwater and breathing with gills to adults living on land and breathing with lungs, also spending part of the time in the water and laying its eggs there. In general, a complete metamorphosis features clearly distinct stages of development, whereas an incomplete metamorphosis features more gradual changes. Birds, fish, spiders, and mammals (D) including humans have simple life cycles with no metamorphoses.

133. C: Either wavelength or frequency can determine the classification of an electromagnetic wave (i.e., radio waves, microwaves, infrared radiation, visible light, ultraviolet radiation, x-rays, gamma rays). The intensity of an electromagnetic wave is independent from its classification. The speed of light is a constant and, as such, is what allows either wavelength or frequency to describe the wave.

134. C: All three laws of motion are operating, but the third law (forces come in equal and opposite pairs) best explains the motion. The first law (inertia) is shown from the fact that the balloon doesn't move until a force acts upon it. The second law (F = ma) is shown because you can see the force and the acceleration. The force comes from the contraction of the rubber balloon. The stretched rubber exerts a force on the air inside the balloon. This causes the air to accelerate in accordance with the second law. You can't see this acceleration because the air is invisible and because it is the air inside the balloon being pushed out through the opening that the balloon is exerting a force on. However, the air being pushed out of the balloon exerts an equal and opposite force on the balloon (this is Newton's third law), which causes the balloon to accelerate in the direction it did.

135. C: In a pond, plants produce oxygen as a byproduct of photosynthesis. During eutrophication, plants die and decompose, causing increased levels of carbon dioxide. Fish cannot relocate from the pond, and they cannot live without oxygen, so they would die.

136. D: Since the atomic number of this isotope is 92, the atom contains 92 protons. Since the mass number is 238, the atom contains 238 protons and neutrons. Since the difference between 238 and 92 is 146, the atom contains 146 neutrons.

137. C: In a uniform gravitational field, such as occurs near Earth's surface, an object will move like a point mass located at the center of mass. However, this does not necessarily mean that the geometrical center of an object is the same as its center of mass, depending on its shape, design and mass distribution. The center of mass of a sphere or cube is at its geometric center because you can imagine the sphere as consisting of a large number of point masses located at certain points in space. Multiplying the point masses by their location and dividing by the total mass gives the center of mass. Statement I is not true because the space station may not be completely symmetrical. Statement III is true because the space station is undergoing uniform circular motion around Earth. If the orbit had been elliptical, this would not be true because the speed would have changed depending on the station's position. However, even though the speed is constant in a circular orbit, the velocity is not. Since velocity has a direction associated with it, and the space station is moving in a circular path, its velocity is constantly changing.

138. A: The body's main fuel is the simple sugar glucose. Complex carbohydrates provide the body with sustained energy by slowly breaking down into glucose.

139. A: Most organic molecules are not highly soluble in water. A low melting point, covalent bonds, and high flammability are all characteristics of organic molecules. Organic molecules are those that contain carbon atoms, with a few exceptions. Organic molecules tend to be less soluble in water than inorganic salts. They are good at forming unique structures and there are many organic compounds. Examples of organic compounds include hydrocarbons, carbohydrates, lipids, and proteins.

140. C: Unlike the other choices, a tectonic plate shift is a natural geologic process and not a result of human activity. In contrast, human activities are responsible for many forms of ocean destruction. As wetlands are degraded or lost, many ecosystems and species are also lost, interrupting their respective food webs. Food webs within the oceans are further disrupted by pollution and climate change, which alter water temperatures and conditions. The diminishment of coral reefs reduces the ocean's natural water filtration and destroys critical habitats used for breeding and feeding.

141. C: The main human-caused reason for "dead zones" in portions of oceans and lakes that normally host abundant aquatic life is the use of chemical fertilizers. These fertilizers, which are high in nitrogen and phosphorous, enter lakes and rivers in water runoff and become concentrated in certain areas. This concentration, called eutrophication, eventually depletes the water's oxygen levels and renders it incapable of supporting life.

142. C: A physical change occurs when water condenses. The only thing formed during condensation is new intermolecular bonds. Therefore, no new covalent bonds form (B). The only time new atoms form is during a nuclear reaction (A). The water molecule is not ionizing, so no new ionic bonds form (D).

143. B: Albert Einstein is known for both the special theory of relativity and the general theory of relativity. Thomas Edison was an inventor best known for inventing the light bulb and phonograph.

144. B: A trace fossil shows evidence of existence but is not an organism itself. A trace fossil can be contrasted with a body fossil, which has been formed from an organism. Other examples of trace fossils include eggs, nests, burrows, borings, and coprolites (fossilized feces). A mouse jaw and a shark tooth are examples of body fossils. A cast of a skull is a replica and neither a body nor a trace fossil.

145. A: Fish may die suddenly after heavy rains due to the lower pH leading to high levels of substances such as aluminum in the water. Over time, acid rain may slowly remove nutrients from the forest soil, weakening defenses of trees, making them more vulnerable to diseases and pests. Excess nitrogen may lead to overgrowth of algae in areas where rivers enter the ocean. Acid rain may slowly deteriorate buildings and monuments made from stone containing calcium carbonate.

146. B: The trend within any column of the periodic table is that electronegativity decreases going down the column.

147. B: The Earth's environment consists of the atmosphere (the air we breathe), the hydrosphere (water), and the lithosphere (the land).

148. B: Cells are the basic units of life, and all organisms have them. Some organisms like bacteria have just a single cell, while complex organisms like humans have hundreds of trillions. Prokaryotes do not have organelles Not all organisms have tissues, groups of cells that make up connective tissue, muscle tissue, etc. Finally, only some types of cells, including plant cells, have cell walls d.

149. C: In 2.4×10^4 years, 50% of the substance will have decayed. In another half-life, half of this will be gone, or 75%. 87.5% represents 3 half-lives, or a total of $3 \times 2.4 \times 10^4$ years = 7.2×10^4 years.

150. D: This graph shows the effect of increasing the amount of solute in a solution on both vapor pressure lowering and boiling point elevation. The change in vapor pressure is a decrease due to the label of *vapor pressure lowering*. As the amount of solute increases, the amount the vapor pressure is lowered continually increases. Increasing the solute decreases the vapor pressure. Increasing the solute also increases the amount the boiling point is elevated. Increasing the solute increases the boiling point of the solution.

151. C: Plants reproduce both asexually and sexually. Asexual reproduction occurs through runners that some plants extend to root new growth, through plant cuttings being rooted in water and then planted, and through grafts. Plants reproduce sexually through fertilization, wherein plant gametes combine, contributing chromosomes from both sides, similarly to how animals mate. The other answer options are correct.

152. C: Catalysts lower the energy barrier between products and reactants and thus increase the reaction rate. Catalysts do not change the thermodynamic position of equilibrium, reaction temperature, or product purity on their own.

153. B: Water moves more slowly downstream of a dam. This results in less aeration and diffusion and lowers the dissolved oxygen content in the water.

154. C: Cytokinins stimulate cell division (cytokinesis) and have been found to delay senescence (aging). They are often sprayed on cut flowers and fruit to prolong their shelf life.

155. B: A guyot is defined as a seamount with a flattened top. The term "seamount" refers to any undersea volcano that is more than 1,000 meters tall. Undersea troughs are called trenches, and undersea mountain chains are called mid-ocean ridges.

156. C: As the temperature drops to –5 °C, the water vapor condenses to a liquid, and then to a solid. The partial pressure of a solid is much less than that of the corresponding gas. The argon is still a gas at –5 °C, so almost all the pressure in the cylinder is due to argon. Since the partial pressure of the water decreases as it turns to a solid, the totally pressure in the cylinder also decreases.

157. B: The most severe mass extinction event in Earth's history was the Permian-Triassic Event. It occurred approximately 251.4 million years ago, and resulted in the extinction of 96 percent of all marine species and 70 percent of terrestrial vertebrate species.

158. B: Hurricanes are primarily formed because of the temperature difference between the oceans and the atmospheric air. The oceans heat up during the summer months and once they climb above 80 degrees Fahrenheit, the conditions are ideal for a hurricane. Evaporation of the warm water forms clouds, which then expand into storm clouds. Atmospheric winds help push the storm over warmer waters, allowing it to grow. A hurricane will die if introduced to cold waters or cut off from a water source.

159. C: Producers always form the base of an energy pyramid as the first trophic level. Each successive level receives about 10% of the energy from the previous level. In this energy pyramid, the second trophic level receives 10% of 6,000 or 600 kilocalories per square meter per year. The third trophic level receives 10% of 600, or 60 kilocalories per square meter per year.

160. B: Epiphytes are plants that grow in the canopy of trees, and the tropical rain forest has a rich canopy because of its density and extensive moisture.